inside the Jewelry Box

VOLUME 3

A Collector's Guide to

Costume Jewelry

*Identification
and
Values*

Ann Mitchell Pitman

COLLECTOR BOOKS
A Division of Schroeder Publishing Co., Inc.

Cover design by Beth Summers
Book design by Beth Ray
Cover photography by Charles R. Lynch

COLLECTOR BOOKS
P.O. Box 3009
Paducah, Kentucky 42002-3009

www.collectorbooks.com

Copyright © 2009 Ann Mitchell Pitman

The current values in this book should be used only as a guide. They are
not intended to set prices, which vary from one section of the country to another. Auction prices as well as dealer prices vary greatly and are affected by
condition as well as demand. Neither the author nor the publisher assumes
responsibility for any losses that might be incurred as a result of consulting
this guide.

Searching for a Publisher?

We are always looking for people knowledgeable within their fields. If you
feel that there is a real need for a book on your collectible subject and have a
large comprehensive collection, contact Collector Books.

Proudly printed and bound in the
United States of America

Contents

Acknowledgments

Over the years I have met a great many collectors, both in person and over the internet. All of these collectors have been willing to share their knowledge and their jewelry with me in my quest to learn. Some have gone so far as to send me gifts in appreciation.

One such gift was the Claudette emerald green Easter Egg pin, sent to me by my friend Jennifer Lynn Edie, whose website can be found at jltimelessjewelry.com. I was shocked and thrilled when I opened the package from her to discover this long sought after pin. Her note said, "I read in your first book that you couldn't wait to find the pin that matched your green earrings. Here it is, a gift for you." It is a real beauty, as you will see when you turn the pages and find it. Thank you Jennifer Lynn, you know I love it!

My dear friend Donna Burns continues to hold my hand and let me bend her ear, and I don't know what I would do without her friendship. We have had a special friendship for nearly 20 years, and I look forward to the next 20.

My daddy starting sending me little packages filled with jewelry he picked up on his trips to flea markets or antique shops. He calls me to tell me about his finds, and one time he called to say my mother had pilfered one of the pins. Instead of being mad, I was very happy about this, knowing they both now had a better appreciation for this hobby that fills my life with pleasure. But the day he called and said he had added several pins to his own collection, I knew I had truly hooked him! Daddy loves flower pins, most especially rose bud pins. He has an amazing collection by Giovanni with a dozen varieties of the same design, like a gold rose with silver leaves, a silver rose with gold leaves, a gold rose with silver thorns, and so on. He has found some really great jewelry, including my most favorite red rhinestone flower. And though now my mom gets plenty of the jewelry he finds, I still manage to get my share of it. I keep it in the enormous wooden jewelry box he gave me, so it will forever be known as "daddy's jewelry" and will be passed down to future generations of rhinestone queens.

During the Vintage Costume Jewelry and Fashion convention I attended in Providence, Rhode Island, in October 2007, I met an amazing variety of collectors, and several of them were kind enough to allow me to photograph a few of the beauties from their collections. Most of these pieces you will find in the chapter on Quality, because these are serious collectors with unbelievable jewelry. Cheryl Killmer was the first to let me play in her jewelry box, and we passed many an email back and forth when I got home and began working with the photos. Thank you, Cheryl, I know I was a huge pest but I hope this book with your incredible jewelry in it was worth it.

Kay Heino came in and I couldn't believe all of this sensational jewelry was from her own personal collection. Judy Miller brought me some jewelry I had only dreamed of one day holding in my sweaty little hands, and Laney Ortega popped in for a visit wearing mind boggling Eisenberg jewels and carrying a Calvaire purse. I promptly made her take all of it off to photograph. Cynthia Fore Miller came in wearing another spectacular Eisenberg brooch and under the camera it went, along with a tremendous bracelet made by fellow attendee Dinah Hoyt Taylor, whose jewelry creations you will see featured in the Contemporary chapter. And of course Mary Ann Docktor-Smith brought me some fascinating pieces from her collection, and even wrote book-worthy descriptions. Jayne Spencer brought me some gorgeous jewels, and even helped me load my car. Sherry James and Robin Valiunas stopped by looking for their friends and I took the jewelry right off of them to photograph. Lisa Boydstun had some incredible parures that had to be included. Thank you, Kay, Judy, Laney, Dinah, Cynthia, Mary Ann, Jayne, Sherry, Robin, and Lisa, your input will make this book another great success! Cackle on!

During the convention, I won an impressive fruit bracelet designed by Annie Navetta. When I returned home, she sent me a surprise box with one of her newest bead creations and a necklace to match my glorious fruit bracelet. My thanks to Annie and all of the people who dropped out of the bidding for this tasty creation! It looks like it was made just for me, and is a perfect fit.

Jan Gaughan offered her assistance and I snatched the opportunity to feature some of her Forbidden Fruit collection. I have never been able to snag a beehive, caterpillar, or a butterfly, but she has, and she repeatedly took photos to get them just right. Thanks, Jan.

James Katz of James Katz Vintage Jewelry and Accessories has an archive filled with Calvaire jewelry photographs. He kindly allowed me to borrow the photos for my chapter on Calvaire. Thank you, Jim.

Kim Paff of www.kimlovesvintage.com shared photographs of her Kunio Matsumoto and copper jewelry, and I appreciate the opportunity to share this unusual jewelry with you. Thanks, Kim.

Elizabeth Rowlands of www.emcity.com has a fabulous collection of Pennino jewelry and she has allowed me to share these photos in the chapter on Pennino. Thank you, Beth.

My dear friend Davida Baron has an eye for the best of the best, and a museum worthy collection. She worked day in and day out with me to get some of her jewels photographed to add to the book, and I gratefully acknowledge her input and support. At times I felt like I might need to add her name as co-author; I greatly value her friendship. Thanks, Davida!

When I first saw the new cover of this book, I was thrilled beyond belief. I didn't think that the fine people at Collector Books could improve on the marvelous cover they did for my second book, but they proved me wrong. I sent them the jewelry, and told them I wanted a purple cover, and they fulfilled my dreams. My thanks go to out to my editor Gail Ashburn, assistant editor Amy Sullivan, cover stylist Beth Summers, and book designer Beth Ray for doing a phenomenal job with this book. Most especially, I would like to thank Billy Schroeder for taking another chance on me.

The kind people at Gaudin Jaguar loaned me a sporty convertible to have my photo made in, and my thanks go out to them. If you are in Vegas, stop and visit them on West Sahara.

This has been an incredible year for me, which included moving to fabulous Las Vegas, getting stuck in the elevator on the 36th floor after a Christmas party beautifully hosted by Linda Johansen James, and final-ly being rescued by the smartest man in Vegas, Max James. I proudly watched my daughter graduate from law school and pass the bar exam. I got to go back home to South Carolina and have a book launch party with my family and friends at the greatest vintage jewelry store, The Vintage Jewelry Shop, in historic downtown Greer, with my friends Peter Tripp and Harold Baker. They also allowed me to photograph some jewelry from their personal collections and their store stock. My dear friend Laurel Ladd Ciotti even drove up from Florida to share a glass of wine and some gossip. We got to sit in chairs that had belonged to Tammy Faye Baker and were treated like royalty. I even made it to California and decided, hey, I *do* like it there!

This book would not have been possible without the assistance of so many people who shared their jewelry and their photographs, and I hope you enjoy seeing this exceptional collection. I also fired off a great many emails to friends trying to verify information, or ask for assistance in some other way. Kathy Flood and I have been email friends for over a decade and she seemed to be ready at the drop of a hat to answer my emails. Thanks, Kathy. And if I left anyone's name out, please accept my apologies, it was not intentional.

But the best part has been starting a new adventure with my oldest and dearest friend; I would not be what I am today with his help. Tony, you continue to make my life exciting and fun, and you make me feel loved every single day. Here's to faith and new beginnings.

Photo by Tony C. Pitman

Introduction

The first installment of my column, "Inside the Jewelry Box," ran in February 1997. Each column was written to share a little bit of information about different jewelry companies and designers, chat about repairs and reproductions, and suggest books for the reference library. Most columns ran around 1,000 words, and I wrote them as if I were chatting with fellow collectors of vintage costume jewelry.

This book is the third book in the series, and it features different columns than the previous two books. It also features, for the most part, completely different jewelry, without repeats. Oh, you may run across a repeat or two, but if you have the previous two books, then you will see that perhaps I showed the emerald green Mazer bracelet again, but since I found the earrings to match, then I had to show it as a set. Or I may have found a piece of jewelry in a different color, such as the Les Bernard mechanical flower pins and wanted to share them with you. Generally, unless I suffered from forgetfulness, which is entirely possible, there are no repeats in any of the books so far, besides the aforementioned examples.

You will notice that the jewelry was photographed from different collections, just like the previous books. Some of these people I met for the first time when photographing their jewelry but now I call them friends. I received a review one time that complained that I featured the jewelry of my "friends," but I ask you, who else's jewelry *would* I feature? A lot of the photographs came from different collectors but any mistakes with identifying jewelry, values, or owners are all mine. These collectors have wonderful jewelry that needed to be shared.

Another thing that is mentioned in reviews is the pricing done for each book. The jewelry that is not mine, except for my parents jewelry, is from the collections or inventory of dealers, and the prices are the ones they had on their tags at the time of their being photographed. I stand behind all of the prices listed, and ask that you remember that a piece of jewelry that sells on the east coast brings a far different price from a piece found in a small town or one found in an antique mall in California.

You will note that this book has more photographs of the reverse side of jewelry than in my previous two books. You can learn a lot by seeing how the jewelry is made, and seeing the backs is very important in learning about different companies' styles of designs. It is very useful in helping to attribute unsigned pieces, so I have included a lot of reverse photographs for you.

This book has been arranged, as have the first two, into chapters that feature extended information on particular companies or designers, followed by plastic jewelry, quality jewelry, and then jewelry broken down by category. There are a few websites mentioned that were not in the first two books, followed by a listing of all of the websites that were in those books, giving a complete look at what is available for the collector on the internet. If you have a website that you think bears sharing, or know of one I haven't mentioned, simply write to me to be considered for my next book. My email address is annmpitman@yahoo.com and I welcome your letters. I love hearing from readers so please write with any concerns you may have, or jewelry you wish to share or about which you have questions. Enjoy!

Forbidden Fruit

The term "Forbidden Fruit" can have many different meanings, but to collectors of vintage costume jewelry, that term means only one thing: rhinestone encrusted fruit jewelry. And actually, they came in more than just fruit, they also came in a variety of vegetables, and mushrooms, and the most amazing little beehives. There is even a set of butterflies. And a precious little caterpillar.

Not much is known about this line of jewelry. It has been found on original paper cards that say "Forbidden Fruit" at the top, and "Austrian Jewels hand set" at the bottom. Collectors think this jewelry is from the 1950s because of the findings. And the design seems to have been perfect for that era.

Forbidden Fruit jewelry didn't have just an amazing variety of shapes. Take fruit for instance. You could get apples, pears, grapes, lemons and limes, oranges, pineapples, strawberries, cherries, peaches, and even watermelon. Then the color combinations seem endless. Take grapes. You can have red grapes with red rhinestones, green grapes with green rhinestones, pink grapes with pink rhinestones, and blue grapes with blue rhinestones. Or you could have white grapes with green rhinestones or blue rhinestones or champagne colored rhinestones. How about black grapes with black rhinestones? But that isn't the limit of the grapes. These were made with what looks like clear, colored Lucite. But they also came in opaque colors of the same Lucite and many of these opaque grapes have white rhinestones. Not clear, but true white. And not just white rhinestones. There are even colors like opaque peach grapes with bright peachy rhinestones.

And they didn't forget we need our vegetables too. Forbidden Fruit came in corn, radishes, mushrooms, tomatoes, eggplant, pumpkins, carrots, and bell peppers. There are even a couple of melon-shaped unidentifiable fruit/vegetables; one short and squat, the other tall and rounded. The radishes, carrots, bell peppers, and eggplants are extremely rare and can command prices over $200.00, while most pieces sell for $50.00 to $125.00, with sets bringing from $125.00 up.

The butterflies are nice, but don't seem to have the same cachet as the fruit and vegetables. The beehives are fabulous, though, encrusted with rhinestones and featuring a tiny gold colored honey bee coming in for a

More rare Forbidden Fruit jewelry line with butterflies, also available in a variety of colors, $125.00 – 225.00. Jan Gaughan collection/Photo courtesy of Jan Gaughan, Eclectic Vintage collection

landing. And the caterpillar is spectacular, crawling away to enjoy a nice piece of fruit or a vegetable.

For those people who didn't relish their fruit totally encrusted with rhinestones, there is a line of the fruits and vegetables which are only dotted with only five or ten little rhinestones, just to highlight them. There are also examples without any stones at all

All of these fruit and vegetables pins are quite sought after by collectors, who will pay a premium for those pieces they covet to add to their collection. Recent auctions showed tomato earrings netting a final bid of $211.50 in March of 2007; a pair of pineapple earrings had a final whopping bid of $406.00 in August 2007. And a pumpkin pin with the highlight rhinestones made a final bid of $83.00 in September 2007. All of the above were at online auctions, with no buyers premiums added, those are true bids.

I looked through many of my jewelry reference books searching for more information on this line of jewelry, and couldn't find more than a single photo in any of the books. Except for my two books, which both feature this jewelry. No surprise there, since I am nuts for this type of jewelry!

My thanks go to Jan Gaughan who shared her collection of Forbidden Fruit with me. Pieces from her archive collection will not have measurements. All of the photos of her jewelry from her collection are courtesy of Jan Gaughan, Eclectic Vintage collection. Visit her website at www.eclecticvintage.com.

Forbidden Fruit mushroom came in different colors, $95.00 – 175.00. Jan Gaughan collection/Photo courtesy of Jan Gaughan, Eclectic Vintage collection

Superb and very rare Forbidden Fruit bee hive with hovering bee, like all of this line of jewelry, it comes in a variety of colors, $150.00 – 225.00. Jan Gaughan collection/Photo courtesy of Jan Gaughan, Eclectic Vintage collection

Opaque Forbidden Fruit oranges in orange with white rhinestones, set with pin and earrings, **$125.00 – 175.00.** Jan Gaughan collection/Photo courtesy of Jan Gaughan, Eclectic Vintage collection

This set of strawberry Forbidden Fruit is so beautiful that it actually looks quite juicy in person. The pin is 2" x 1½" and the earrings are 1⅛" tall, all Forbidden Fruit jewelry is unsigned, **$125.00 – 175.00.** Author collection

Raspberry set of pin, earrings, and scatter pin in fuchsia, **$175.00 – 225.00.** Jan Gaughan archive collection/Photo courtesy of Jan Gaughan, Eclectic Vintage collection

Berries set with small scatter pin and earrings, **$125.00 – 175.00.** Jan Gaughan archive collection/Photo courtesy of Jan Gaughan, Eclectic Vintage collection

Lemon pin and earrings set, pin is 2" x 1⅓", earrings are 1⅛", **$125.00 – 175.00.** Author collection

Berries set with pin and earrings, **$125.00 – 175.00.** Jan Gaughan archive collection/Photo courtesy of Jan Gaughan, Eclectic Vintage collection

Grapes set of pin and earrings in opaque orange with white rhinestones, **$125.00 – 175.00.** Jan Gaughan archive collection/Photo courtesy of Jan Gaughan, Eclectic Vintage collection

Four different grapes scatter pins, **$75.00 – 125.00 each.** Jan Gaughan archive collection/Photo courtesy of Jan Gaughan, Eclectic Vintage collection

Two different shades of grapes pins, one is medium pink and the other is a very pale pink, with white rhinestones, pin is 1¾", $75.00 – 125.00 each. Author collection

Red grapes scatter pin with ruby red rhinestones, enameled leaves, 1¼", $45.00 – 65.00. Author collection

A pair of grapes earrings, one with white rhinestones set in peach, the other with orange rhinestones set in orange, earrings are the exact same size as the scatter pins on page 9, 1¼", $65.00 – 95.00 for the earrings, $125.00 – 175.00 with the matching grapes pins. Author collection

Shades of blue grapes, white with blue rhinestones and dark blue with blue rhinestones, 1¼", $65.00 – 95.00 for the earrings, $125.00 – 175.00 with the matching pins. Author collection

White grapes earrings with white rhinestones and with champagne rhinestones, 1¼", $65.00 – 95.00 for the earrings, $125.00 – 175.00 with the matching pins. Author collection

Pear fruit pin with champagne colored rhinestones, 1¾", $95.00 – 125.00. Author collection

Pear fruit pin in black with black rhinestones, 1¾", **$95.00 – 125.00.** Jan Gaughan archive collection/Photo courtesy of Jan Gaughan, Eclectic Vintage collection

Black fruit with black rhinestones, **$95.00 – 125.00.** Jan Gaughan archive collection/Photo courtesy of Jan Gaughan, Eclectic Vintage collection

Black lemon pin with black rhinestones, 2" x 1¾", **$95.00 – 125.00.** Jan Gaughan archive collection/Photo courtesy of Jan Gaughan, Eclectic Vintage collection

Pair of multicolored rhinestone berry scatter pins, 1⅛", **$95.00 – 125.00.** Author collection

Berries earrings in fuchsia, could also be an apple, 1", **$65.00 – 95.00.** Author collection

Oranges with orange rhinestones earrings, 1⅛", **$65.00 – 95.00.** Author collection

Mixed fruit pins, lemon, **$65.00**; apple and lime **$125.00** each. Jan Gaughan archive collection/Photo courtesy of Jan Gaughan, Eclectic Vintage collection

Pineapple with champagne colored rhinestones, 2³⁄₁₆" x 1¹⁄₁₆", **$125.00 – 225.00**. Jan Gaughan archive collection/Photo courtesy of Jan Gaughan, Eclectic Vintage collection

This pair of pears of Forbidden Fruit have the rhinestone accents instead of being covered with rhinestones like the previous examples, this could also be a pair of figs, **$125.00 – 225.00**. Jan Gaughan archive collection/Photo courtesy of Jan Gaughan, Eclectic Vintage collection

Caterpillar with clear aurora borealis rhinestones, **$125.00 – 225.00**. Jan Gaughan archive collection/Photo courtesy of Jan Gaughan, Eclectic Vintage collection

Corn with golden rhinestones, 2¼" tall, **$125.00 – 225.00**. Jan Gaughan archive collection/Photo courtesy of Jan Gaughan, Eclectic Vintage collection

Juliana

DeLizza & Elster Juliana jewelry has been on the must-have list for collectors for several years now. Some collectors had always searched for this unsigned jewelry, and it was reasonably priced. Bracelets and necklaces could be found for as little as $25.00 and pins and earrings could be found for around $10.00.

Then one day a collector named Cheryl Killmer shared photos of this bright, showy, and colorful jewelry with her online collecting group, Jewelcollect, also known as JC. Another member had a similar piece that had a small black and gold tag on it reading Juliana, and news about it spread like wildfire.

Killmer seemed to have lit a match under collectors who scrambled to add this now "named" jewelry to their collection. Others who collected it were happy to finally have a name to attribute it to. And once Killmer shared this incredible collection, collectors started fighting over it. Auction prices skyrocketed, dealers could suddenly ask $200.00, $300.00, or even $500.00 for these sets and now get it. I have even seen complete parures priced at $1,500.00 or more.

Killmer then collected the *coup de grace* by finding Frank DeLizza, who was amazed and thrilled to discover that collectors were clamoring after the jewelry made by his family's company, which lead to a group of Juliana collectors and then to a book written by DeLizza.

DeLizza shares stories of over 40 years of manufacturing fashion jewelry, along with photos and drawings. It is interesting to note that while collectors have come to believe that all the five link bracelets and matching pieces were made during the short period of the tagged "Juliana" years in the mid 1960s, in reality this style of jewelry was made as early as 1955 and produced all the way through 1990, when the company closed.

I met Frank DeLizza in Providence, Rhode Island, in October 2007 and he is delightful. As soon as I introduced myself and told him I lived in Las Vegas, he started telling me about the time DeLizza and Elster got an order from a Las Vegas casino to make rhinestone bras for the showgirls in one of their shows. DeLizza said his men fought to be the ones to head out to Vegas to take the measurements! Contact me if you would like to order a copy of his book, *DeLizza and Elster, Memoirs of a Fashion Jewelry Manufacturer*. He will be happy to sign a copy for you.

Design collections now referred to as Juliana start with the bracelets which are identified by the five link construction, the fold-over clasp with a chevron or feathered design, a safety chain, and the backs with rhinestone link chain have a figure 8 "puddling" where the links are turned or bent to hold the design and then soldered. Once a bracelet has been identified, the matching pieces are easy to identify. DeLizza & Elster also made a ton of designs where the bracelet designs are flat or the side hinged cuff bracelets are etched. In truth, DeLizza & Elster was a major manufacturer of fashion jewelry, but it is the style known as Juliana which has captured the attention of collectors. You will note a disparity in the values of the jewelry listed below; there are some sets and some colors which are much more desirable than others, and their values reflect the desirability.

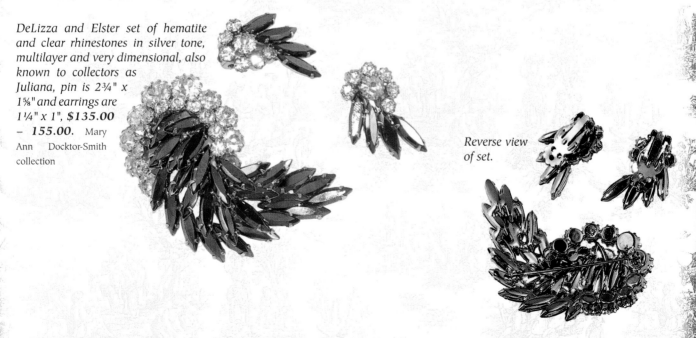

DeLizza and Elster set of hematite and clear rhinestones in silver tone, multilayer and very dimensional, also known to collectors as Juliana, pin is 2¾" x 1⅝" and earrings are 1¼" x 1", $135.00 – 155.00. Mary Ann Docktor-Smith collection

Reverse view of set.

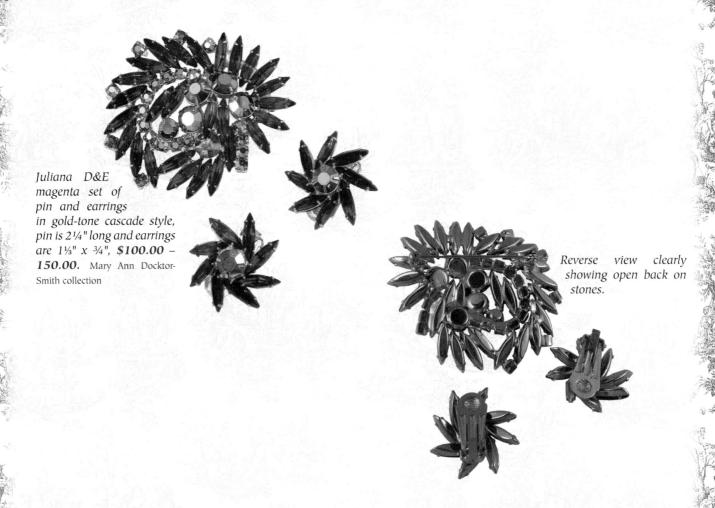

Juliana D&E magenta set of pin and earrings in gold-tone cascade style, pin is 2¼" long and earrings are 1⅓" x ¾", **$100.00 – 150.00.** Mary Ann Docktor-Smith collection

Reverse view clearly showing open back on stones.

Juliana red rhinestone pin and earrings set with prong-set red navettes and pink aurora borealis chatons. Pin is 2½" x 2⅛" and earrings are 1¼" in diameter, **$100.00 – 150.00.** Mary Ann Docktor-Smith collection

Reverse view of set.

This sensational pink and gold parure with necklace, bracelet, brooch, and earrings shows off the
best of D&E design, the tear drop cabochons are pink
striated with gold dust lines, necklace is 16", bracelet
is 7", pin is 3½" x 2", and earrings are 1¼" x¾", **$495.00
– 695.00.** Lisa Boydstun collection

*Five link bracelet in bold and beautiful shades of green with all round prong-set rhinestones
in dark green, pale green, and clear, 7½" x¾", **$125.00– 195.00.*** Author collection

Reverse view showing link construction.

Ruby red two-tiered japanned pin with marquise, pear, and round rhinestones, complete with Juliana black and gold tag, 1¾" x 2½", **$55.00 – 125.00.** Author collection

Reverse view showing japanned finish.

Here is one of the most fun designs in great Mardi Gras colors of purple and green. First this necklace has a great centerpiece drop of nearly 4", it has round clear and aurora borealis rhinestones. Next it has prong-set unfoiled marquise rhinestones in amethyst and blue. And lastly, it has groups of three beads attached together; one clear glass purple, one clear glass green, and then a plastic iridescent purplish-green or greenish-purple bead. Necklace is 15½" long, **$155.00 – 255.00+.** Author collection

Reverse view showing construction.

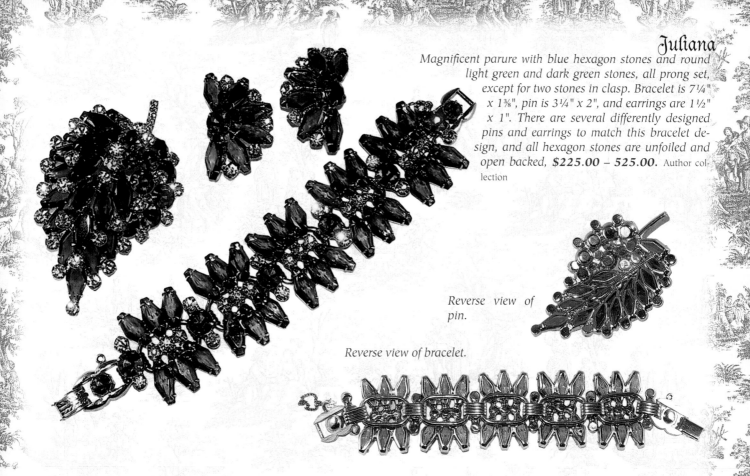

Magnificent parure with blue hexagon stones and round light green and dark green stones, all prong set, except for two stones in clasp. Bracelet is 7¼" x 1⅜", pin is 3¼" x 2", and earrings are 1½" x 1". There are several differently designed pins and earrings to match this bracelet design, and all hexagon stones are unfoiled and open backed, **$225.00 – 525.00.** Author collection

Reverse view of pin.

Reverse view of bracelet.

This splendid little red pin has rhinestones known as keyhole stones, they are four sided with a larger top that tapers to a smaller bottom, the keyhole stones are unfoiled and open backed. Pin is 2½" x 2⅛", and accented with clear rhinestones, **$75.00 – 125.00.** Author collection

Reverse view of pin.

The same pin with Montana blue keyhole stones, light blue stones, and clear aurora borealis stones, 2½" x 2⅛", **$75.00 – 125.00.** Author collection

Reverse view of pin.

This hexagon designed bracelet has brown hexagon rhinestones accented with pale celery green and bright orange stones, all prong set except for stones in clasp. All hexagon stones are unfoiled and open backed, 7¼" x 1⅜", clasp is fold over with chevron design and it has a safety chain, **$95.00 – 165.00.** Author collection

Matching pin to above bracelet with brown hexagon stones, 3⅛" x 2", though pin is identical to the blue hexagon pin on page 17, the size is slightly different because of the manufacture, note design on brown pin curves while blue pin goes straight down at the bottom. The stem is also slightly different; it curves downward with the brown and goes straight with the blue. **$65.00 – 125.00.** Author collection

Earrings with prong-set stones in dark green, medium green, and clear aurora borealis, this style has been vetted through the Discovering Juliana Jewelry group and identified by Frank DeLizza as being a D&E design. Earrings are 1¼" x ⅝", **$25.00 – 35.00.** Author collection

Matching bracelet and earrings in wonderful watermelon stones, five link bracelet is 7" x 1½" and earrings are 1" x 1½", **$395.00 – 595.00.** The Vintage Jewelry collection

Schreiner

My personal collection is filled with gaudy and colorful vintage costume jewelry, and Schreiner of New York certainly fits the bill perfectly. The bad thing is that all of it is so beautiful, prices are high and have been for quite some time. And believe it or not, after nearly 20 years of collecting, I only own one pair of Schreiner fur clips, and didn't know they were Schreiner until I saw a vintage ad featuring them, as they are unmarked.

Quite a bit of Schreiner jewelry is signed but they also made quite a bit that is unsigned. Like many other companies, Schreiner made jewelry for other designers who would usually put paper tags on the jewelry, or their name. This accounts for those pieces collectors spot and feel certain are Schreiner until they turn it over and see the mark of a company such as Adele Simpson or Christian Dior.

Schreiner jewelry has certain characteristics enabling collectors to identify unsigned pieces. By viewing the back of a piece of jewelry, you can see the hook and eye construction they used. Schreiner also used inverted stones and a crimped mounting. Their jewelry designs are rarely flat, most are highly domed. Other characteristics include the use of their signature keystone rhinestone, which were extra long tapered baguettes, and their use of unusual color combinations. Maryanne Dolan, author of *Collecting Colored and Rhinestone Jewelry*, calls this their "sometimes bizarre color combinations" but they somehow seem to work. Nancy Schiffer has a wonderful book titled *Rhinestones!* that is chock full of gorgeous Schreiner jewelry.

Henry Schreiner came to America from Bavaria, Germany, and after working in several different fields, he started Schreiner New York in 1939 and it remained in business until 1977. Following his death in 1951, his daughter and her husband kept the company going. The Schreiner family knew what worked and made jewelry that today remains as stunning and exuberant as the day it was made. Their ruffled design keystone brooch was so popular they made it in a great variety of colors, each incredibly beautiful.

Author Kathy Flood loves Schreiner jewelry. "Schreiner pieces are almost always outstanding, always beautifully done, so you're usually attracted to them right away. When unsigned, they don't always shout Schreiner immediately, so when at last you notice the reverse set jewels and it dawns on you that you love this piece because it's Schreiner, you have to laugh at yourself. As soon as you know it's Schreiner, you realize it couldn't have been anything else. Naturally, I'm partial to Schreiner figurals, but like anyone else, I'd never pass up one of the company's ruffle effect masterpieces," she says. Her new book, *Warman's Costume Jewelry Figurals, Identification and Price Guide*, was published by Krause in 2007.

Many companies made a mix of jewelry that today is, to put it nicely, not all very attractive. Even the greats like Haskell, Hobé, and Eisenberg could come up with an ugly design. But ugly is one word that will never be used with a Schreiner design, and that is one reason the prices will continue to climb.

Schreiner trembler bug pin with art glass body, this little fellow is signed "Schreiner New York" and measures 2 x 1½", **$155.00 – 225.00.** Cheryl Killmer collection

View of signature.

Reverse view.

Unsigned Schreiner parure with art glass cabochons and mint green opaque navettes, necklace 16½" x 1¼", bracelet 8" x 1¾", earrings 1½" x 1¼", **$525.00 – 600.00.** Cheryl Killmer collection

Unsigned Schreiner brooch and earrings of opaque yellow thin navettes in a ruffled design with yellow baguettes, gold-plated metal, and hook-and-eye construction, brooch 2¼" x 2", earrings 1⅛" x 1", **$200.00 – 250.00.** Cheryl Killmer collection

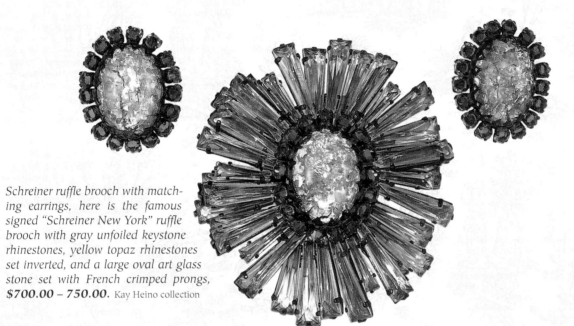

Schreiner ruffle brooch with matching earrings, here is the famous
signed "Schreiner New York" ruffle
brooch with gray unfoiled keystone
rhinestones, yellow topaz rhinestones
set inverted, and a large oval art glass
stone set with French crimped prongs,
$700.00 – 750.00. Kay Heino collection

Close up view of mark.

Reverse view of brooch and earrings.

Barclay vs. McClelland Barclay

Barclay jewelry suffers from mistaken identity. It is a simple misunderstanding, but it could be a very costly one for uninformed collectors. The Barclay Jewelry company was incorporated in the 1940s, and closed during the 1950s, and was located in Providence, Rhode Island. Their jewelry line comprised an affordable alternative to more expensive fashion and costume jewelry of that era.

Barclay designs extend from very simple shapes, such as a daisy with a clear rhinestone center, to the more elaborate designs reminiscent of Hollycraft. Barclay used pleasing combinations of pastel stones such as lavender and blue with these designs, and framed the designs with a twisted gold-tone frame. The jewelry has a substantial feel to it. It is the combination and quality of stones that draws the appreciative eye.

Many Barclay designs were extremely simple, such as the plain gold-tone squiggle or figure eight jewelry, which sadly languish in showcases. The confusion comes in when the few stars of the Barclay line are mistaken for the jewelry by McClelland Barclay, or when uninformed dealers or collectors see the Barclay signature and believe it is the more desirable and rare McClelland Barclay.

McClelland Barclay was a jewelry designer called to serve in World War 11, who was unfortunately killed in action. His jewelry was manufactured by Rice Weiner, who coincidentally also manufactured the line of Barclay jewelry. His jewelry designs have a strong Art Deco feel to them, bold heavy designs highly sought by collectors, highly expensive too. His jewelry is rare, it was only made for six years before the war. It is marked most often with his complete name, McClelland Barclay. But smaller pieces of his jewelry can be found with his distinct font style saying only Barclay. You must be familiar with the McClelland Barclay signature to recognize the difference between the two companies.

Barclay designs are marked only with the name of Barclay in script. The trademark for Barclay is an artist's palette complete with brushes, and the phrase Art In Jewelry. Jewelry can still be found on cards bearing the Barclay mark.

Barclay jewelry can sell for as little as $10.00 for a complete parure to as much as $200.00, maybe $250.00. A McClelland Barclay parure would sell for upwards of $700.00, and I have seen them priced at $3,000.00. Collectors need to be aware of the difference in signatures, to keep themselves and their checkbooks safe.

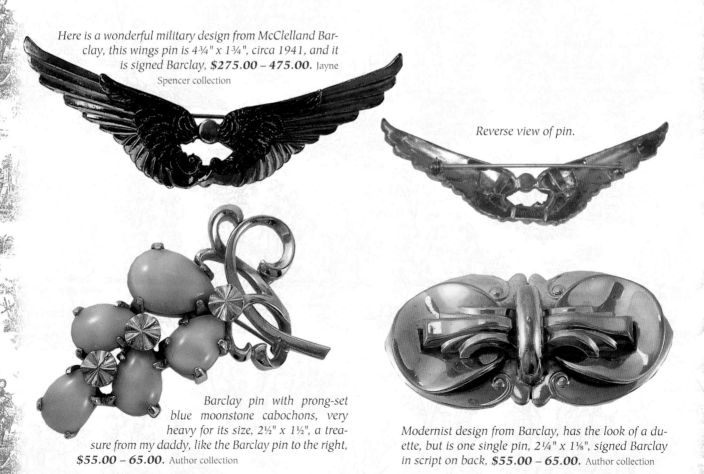

Here is a wonderful military design from McClelland Barclay, this wings pin is 4¾" x 1¾", circa 1941, and it is signed Barclay, **$275.00 – 475.00.** Jayne Spencer collection

Reverse view of pin.

Barclay pin with prong-set blue moonstone cabochons, very heavy for its size, 2½" x 1½", a treasure from my daddy, like the Barclay pin to the right, **$55.00 – 65.00.** Author collection

Modernist design from Barclay, has the look of a duette, but is one single pin, 2¼" x 1⅛", signed Barclay in script on back, **$55.00 – 65.00.** Author collection

Pennino

The Pennino Bros. jewelry company was started in 1926 by three Pennino brothers; Frank, Jack, and Oreste, and remained in business through 1966. Nearly every single piece of jewelry manufactured by this company is stunningly beautiful. Pennino Bros. took the best designs and added the best rhinestones to them and made jewelry so beautiful that collectors today are still clamoring for it.

When I was researching Pennino, I came across this paragraph in the book *Fabulous Costume Jewelry* by Vivienne Becker, published by Schiffer Publishing Ltd.: "Some of the best and strongest costume cocktail jewels were made by an American firm called Pennino. The designs are extraordinary, full of surprises and although very much in the cocktail mood they have an individuality that proclaims the success of costume jewels. The gilt metal, either rose pink or yellow, was cast into strong 1940s shapes of confident and emphatic movement and pride. The compositions and shapes are all finely proportioned, showing a serious and talented approach to the mood of fun and freedom of costume jewels." I really couldn't have said it any better.

Becker's paragraph perfectly expresses the beauty and design of Pennino. Many of their designs are floral or stylized florals with large single stones used as petals, and often accentuated with ribbons and bows. Their abstract designs are also quite popular with collectors.

Like many of their counterparts at the time, Pennino designed jewelry to mimic the real thing of genuine gold, diamonds, emeralds, rubies, and sapphires. One of their designers was Beneditto Panetta who later started his own costume jewelry company, also equally famous with the same high standards of quality and design. Collectors love Pennino and pay premium prices for the beautiful jewelry.

Collector and dealer Elizabeth Rowlands, owner of www.emcity.com agrees. "Whether they're the flamboyant Retro Moderne pieces of the 1940s or the later more delicate pieces, Pennino jewelry is constructed with attention to detail and is infused with sophistication. It's that elegance and real-look that I adore, and their scarcity makes Pennino pieces a great find for collectors. The use of molded, melon shaped stones to simulate moonstones or sapphires is truly charming. Yet, the word 'magic' is what popped out of my mouth the first time I spotted a floral necklace using black matte enamel and rhinestones in rhodium plated settings. Like the pansy necklace in my own collection, these pieces look like black velvet, platinum and diamonds. So elegant!" states Rowlands. Pennino inspires effusive enthusiasm in collectors, and the next time you see a piece of this wonderful jewelry, you too will be inspired.

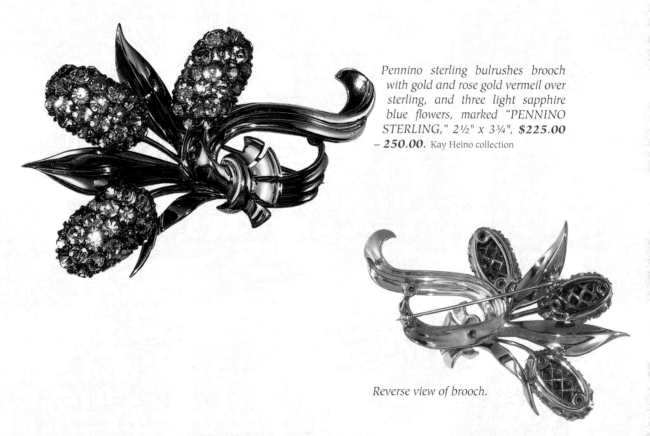

Pennino sterling bulrushes brooch with gold and rose gold vermeil over sterling, and three light sapphire blue flowers, marked "PENNINO STERLING," 2½" x 3¾", $225.00 – 250.00. Kay Heino collection

Reverse view of brooch.

Pennino

My thanks to Elizabeth Rowlands for sharing her collection of Pennino jewelry. Many of the pieces shown below are available at her website at www.emcity.com but others pieces are from her archives collection. Those will not have detailed measurements.

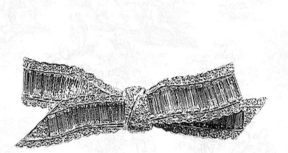

*This bow pin was designed to look like a diamond brooch, like many of the Pennino designs. Pin has clear round and baguette rhinestones, is signed "Pennino," and is 2½" x 1", **$150.00 – 175.00.*** Elizabeth Rowlands collection/Photo courtesy of Elizabeth Rowlands

*Pennino necklace with swirls of clear round and baguette rhinestones, signed, necklace is 16" long and swirl links are 1", **$195.00 – 225.00.*** Elizabeth Rowlands collection/Photo courtesy of Elizabeth Rowlands

*Shooting star brooch with dangling rhinestones, note pavéd heart-shaped leaves, signed, 3½" x 1¾", **$245.00 – 275.00.*** Elizabeth Rowlands collection/Photo courtesy of Elizabeth Rowlands

*Swirl choker with clear rhinestones accented with small amethyst stones, signed "Pennino," necklace is 15½" x 1", **$195.00 – 225.00.*** Elizabeth Rowlands collection/Photo courtesy of Elizabeth Rowlands

Feminine bracelet in silver tone with leaves accented with imitation pearls, signed "Pennino," 7" x ¾", **$150.00 – 175.00.** Elizabeth Rowlands collection/Photo courtesy of Elizabeth Rowlands

Feminine bracelet in gold tone, same as above bracelet, 7" x ¾" **$150.00 – 175.00.** Elizabeth Rowlands collection/Photo courtesy of Elizabeth Rowlands

Lovely design has leaves filled with baguette clear rhinestones, separated by round clusters of clear stones, like rhinestone balls, signed, necklace is 16" x 1", **$195.00 – 225.00.** Elizabeth Rowlands collection/Photo courtesy of Elizabeth Rowlands

Baguette loops necklace with clear round and baguette rhinestones, this necklace has the baguette chain similar to the Mazer Bros. line of jewelry, signed "Pennino," 14½" x 1", **$195.00 – 225.00.** Elizabeth Rowlands collection/Photo courtesy of Elizabeth Rowlands

Pennino

Domed sweetheart earrings with clear rhinestones, signed "Pennino," earrings are ¾" x ¾", $75.00 – 95.00. Elizabeth Rowlands collection/Photo courtesy of Elizabeth Rowlands

Wonderful streamer earrings with long rhinestone dangles, signed, earrings are 3" x ¾", $100.00 – 125.00. Elizabeth Rowlands collection/Photo courtesy of Elizabeth Rowlands

Bracelet with white melon ball cabochons, signed "Pennino," with fold-over clasp and safety chain, 7½" x 1", $130.00 – 150.00. Elizabeth Rowlands collection/Photo courtesy of Elizabeth Rowlands

Pennino clip earrings with carved moonstones on textured gold-tone leaves, signed, earrings are 1⅜" x ¾", $75.00 – 95.00. Elizabeth Rowlands collection/Photo courtesy of Elizabeth Rowlands

Incredibly beautiful floral necklace with clear rhinestone flower links and rhinestone chain, signed "Pennino," necklace is 15½" x 1" at the flower links, **$165.00 – 185.00.** Elizabeth Rowlands collection/Photo courtesy of Elizabeth Rowlands

Pennino lantern pin, signed, with lamp dangling freely, **$65.00 – 95.00.** Elizabeth Rowlands collection/Photo courtesy of Elizabeth Rowlands

Pennino amethyst flower pin in silver tone with pavéd leaf decoration at the top, amethyst stones are collet set, signed, **$195.00 – 250.00.** Elizabeth Rowlands collection/Photo courtesy of Elizabeth Rowlands

Whimsical melon ball set in silver tone with necklace and matching clip earrings, melon balls all hang down to move freely, all signed, **$225.00 – 250.00.** Elizabeth Rowlands collection/Photo courtesy of Elizabeth Rowlands

Canadian Companies

O' Canada! Most of the companies that made the jewelry today's collectors seek were American manufacturers based out of Providence, Rhode Island, but Canadian companies have their own share of the secondary market. Sherman is perhaps the best known, and they are in the midst of a hot streak with collectors right now, with the most colorful pieces going for high prices. But Sherman is not the only Canadian company worth a second look by collectors.

Continental Jewelry is a Canadian company, located in Montreal, Quebec, with great rhinestone jewelry designs. They produced rhinestone jewelry at about the same time as Sherman, and many of their designs stand up to a side by side comparison with Sherman. Continental is not as prolific as many other companies and that makes their jewelry harder to find, but it is worth the effort.

I first discovered Continental when I saw an amazing rhinestone hair clip in the shape of a lovely little bug. It has carved red glass stones and tucks inside a curl for a glamorous accent. I have found two more unusual Continental bug hair clips to add to the collection.

Continental jewelry is very affordable since few collectors know the name. Demi parures can be found for as little as $25.00 up to highs of $50.00. Many of their clear rhinestone pieces are priced less than $5.00, such as earrings. Colored rhinestone pieces are currently starting to see rising prices.

D'Orlan is another Canadian company deserving of a second look and of course many jewelry companies, such as Boucher, Ciro, and Sarah Coventry sold Canadian lines. Look across the border for something new to add to your collection of vintage costume jewelry.

The red is the prettiest bug by far with its carved and frosted red glass body, all stones are prong set. Clip is signed "Continental" and is 1½" long, side wing stones are open backed, $25.00 – 35.00. Author collection

Reverse view of hair clip showing signature.

These two hair clips are nearly identical, this one has a large round lavender stone for its head. **$20.00 – 25.00.**

This hair clip has a small oval pink stone for its head.

What collection of jewelry is complete without a maple leaf pin from Canada? My husband brought me back this pin and the one below from his trip to Vancouver. This leaf pin is made with abalone shell bits, and the box says it is "Glacier Pearle A Jewel of Nature." It is in a box marked "Storrs," which is a department store in Vancouver. Pin is 1¾" x 1½", **$25.00 – 35.00.** Author collection

I was quite surprised when I opened the box and found this pin showing a high stepping mother penguin and two babies, each enameled in black and white and with a green stone eye, the mother has a mother of pearl belly. I have seen this exact design in a pin signed "Boucher." My pin is signed "LP" and in a box marked "Pan Pacific Vancouver." Pin is 1½" x 1½", **$25.00 – 35.00.** Author collection

29

Ann Vien

Horses, jewelry, and dogs. It seems an odd combination, but it completes the circle of one family. Ann-Vien Jewelry Novelties was based in Atlanta, Georgia, one of the few jewelry companies not located in Providence, Rhode Island. It is a company I had researched without success for many years, and then I ran into the great researcher Nancy Dearing Rossbacher, and asked if she could assist me. Her fingers flew, and the next day, the mystery of this company was solved.

Ann-Vien was listed in the Georgia business directory for the first time in 1945, with an address of 291 Peachtree Street. The company, like so many other jewelry companies, was started at the kitchen table of the Viener family. Simon J. Viener was married to Juanelle, who sat at the kitchen table designing jewelry. Simon and his mother Clara were listed in the business directory as the owners, and daughter Sophie V. Green was the secretary. Clara and her husband Leon were Romanian immigrants who arrived in New York in 1908 and eventually made their way down to Georgia, where what is left of the family remains.

A great deal of Ann-Vien jewelry is beaded so it makes sense that Juanelle could sit in the kitchen and make the first jewelry offerings. It appears that everyone in the family worked for the company in their manufacturing facility. They had a very plain showroom off the beaten path, so most likely sold directly to stores, rather than to the average walk-in customer.

Ann-Vien used all types of beads, plastic and glass. Note the earrings that are silver-tone draped metal design. Many of the beads they used were also used by companies such as Hobé, Alice Caviness, and Hattie Carnegie. The necklaces ranged from short, multi-strand necklaces with extenders to necklaces 56" long, allowing the wearer to drape it in many short strands, a medium length pair of strands or as a single very long flapper style necklace. Some jewelry combines rhinestones and beads while others are basically beads. Many earrings have been found signed, while few necklaces or bracelets with signatures are found. Several of the sets shown are clearly matched sets, but only the earrings are marked. Three different marks have been found; the first two with capital letters; the first is "ANN VIEN" and the second is "ANN-VIEN" with a dash inserted. The last is a rarely seen script hang tag reading "Ann-Vien." It is pronounced Ann-Vee-In.

The company name of Ann-Vien came from Simon's daughter from his first marriage, before Juanelle. Her name was Anita Vierner, thus Ann-Vien. The company managed to stay in business until 1961 or 1962, following the death of Simon. His son Michael ran the business while they were being liquidated after Simon's death.

How did this company combine horses, jewelry, and dogs? The Vieners owned horses, two of which were named Vien-Gold and Solid Gold, and designer Juanelle embellished harness gear and riding clothing with rhinestones. Juanelle today lives quietly in a rest home in Georgia. Her son Carl now rescues retired racing greyhounds.

Though this history is brief, there were several hands involved in solving the mystery. Nancy Dearing Rossbacher gleaned what information she could find from the internet and then contacted researcher Beth McLean at the Atlanta History Center, who located the business information. Dearing Rossbacher then contacted all of the Vierners currently living in Georgia, looking for one who might be related to the company and she found Carl, who, though a young child at the time, shared what he remembered of his family and their business. I would like to thank these people for their hard work and willingness to discuss this company, and I am thrilled to finally know who Ann-Vien was, and their brief history. Some of this jewelry was seen in one of my previous books but since the mystery has been solved, they are being shown here to give a more extensive view of this jewelry.

This beautiful aurora borealis purple two-strand necklace and earrings set uses the same beads that Hobé used in some of their designs. The purple ab beads and the pink crystal beads are glass while the white ones are plastic. Necklace is 14" long with a 2½" extender, and signed clip earrings are 1½", $150.00 – 195.00. Author collection

*Red and black glass three-strand bead necklace and earrings set, necklace is 13" long with a 2½" extender, and signed clip earrings are 1½" tall, **$85.00 – 115.00.** Author collection*

*Pink, black, and purple art glass beaded necklace and earrings set, necklace is 56" long allowing you to make a variety of strand combinations with it, signed clip earrings are 1½" long, a very beautiful set in person, **$150.00 – 195.00.** Author collection*

*Clear crystal and filigree beaded necklace and earrings set, necklace is 54" long while signed clip earrings are 1½", note crystal beads are multi-faceted and six sided, **$135.00 – 155.00.** Author collection*

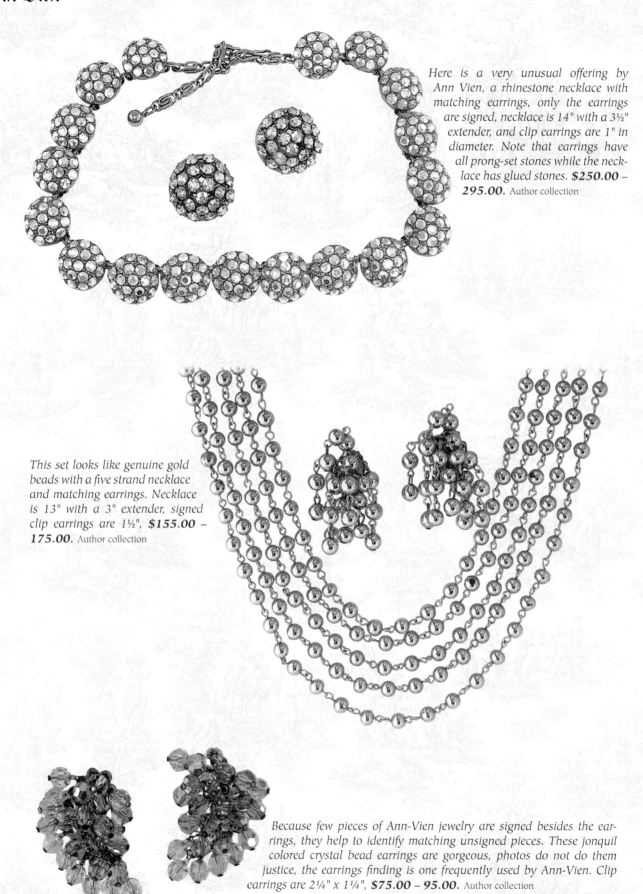

Here is a very unusual offering by Ann Vien, a rhinestone necklace with matching earrings, only the earrings are signed, necklace is 14" with a 3½" extender, and clip earrings are 1" in diameter. Note that earrings have all prong-set stones while the necklace has glued stones. **$250.00 – 295.00.** Author collection

This set looks like genuine gold beads with a five strand necklace and matching earrings. Necklace is 13" with a 3" extender, signed clip earrings are 1½", **$155.00 – 175.00.** Author collection

Because few pieces of Ann-Vien jewelry are signed besides the earrings, they help to identify matching unsigned pieces. These jonquil colored crystal bead earrings are gorgeous, photos do not do them justice, the earrings finding is one frequently used by Ann-Vien. Clip earrings are 2¼" x 1¼", **$75.00 – 95.00.** Author collection

This is a stunning example of saphiret stones in clip earrings, the cabochon glass stone is pinkish tan with flashes of aqua blue inside. Signed earrings are 1" x ⅝" with a depth of nearly ½", **$95.00 – 125.00.** Author collection

Pewter colored imitation pearl clip earrings are signed and accented with rhinestone rhondelles, 1½" x 1", **$45.00 – 55.00.** Author collection

Small blue beads with aurora borealis purple beads make up this signed clip earring design, 1" x 1", **$20.00 – 25.00.** Author collection

These are one of the few Ann Vien designs I have seen with neither rhinestones nor beads, clip earrings are signed, 1¼" x 1", **$10.00 – 15.00.** Author collection

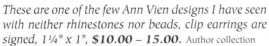

Calvaire

Nancy Dearing Rossbacher is an editor of *North South Trader's Civil War Magazine*, and is a topnotch researcher. After seeing the successful lengths she went to for her research, I spoke with her about assisting me in a search for the true story of Calvaire, Inc. I knew very little, only what had been printed in other books, such as the Brunialti books. The Brunialtis were the first ones to call Ray Mr. Calish, and speculate about he and his wife owning an importing company. But Nancy Dearing Rossbacher was the one who discovered that Ray Calish was not Mr. Calish, but rather, Miss Rachel C. Calish, and the wildfire she started took off.

Dearing Rossbacher discovered that Rachel C. Calish had been born in San Francisco in April of 1885. She found records showing that Calish worked as a bookkeeper for a tailor, moving on to managing a San Francisco department store and then as a buyer for I. Magnin. She also uncovered the fact that Calish traveled frequently on luxury ocean liners, from New York to France and England, an incredible 32 voyages beginning in 1920.

In 1925, Calish started her own business with co-owner Stella Aronson. They were listed as importers, with Aronson being the president and Calish being the secretary treasurer, and they were located in New York at 389 5th Avenue.

Calish and Aronson traveled a great deal, Aronson making 40 round trips over the years between Europe and New York. The name Calvaire is still somewhat of a mystery, if you combine the first part of Calish's name with the first part of Aronson's name, you get "cal" and "aire" without the "v." Perhaps they picked up the name in France, where they traveled so extensively. The French "calvaire" translated into English means "ordeal." Both women had suffered the death of parents at an early age and perhaps the name had meaning for them in that way. Either way, the name has a lovely ring to it.

When looking over the jewelry marked Calvaire, there is no set style or "look" to Calvaire jewelry. I speculated years ago that the buyers simply bought what appealed to them as they wandered through the manufacturers buying rooms. There is a good deal of jewelry found with amethyst colored rhinestones in it, and most of the jewelry is large sized. They leaned toward figurals and flowers, and liked bold stones. If you looked at the jewelry without knowing the mark, you would think that it represented about 10 different companies, because even among, say the animal figurals, they all have a completely different style.

Most of the jewelry is marked "Calvaire" with the "C" stretching out under the "a" and "l." Some is also marked "Sterling." Signatures have been found in both script and block letters. And not just jewelry has been found with the Calvaire mark, but also compacts, purses, and scarves. The purses have tags reading "Made in France for Calvaire of New York."

Perhaps these women imported clothing and only had a few pieces to select from at the fashion houses they visited. Perhaps each only bought what they liked during these travels, since they rarely traveled together. Perhaps one liked flowers and one did not, one liked amethyst and the other did not. Either way, these ladies left behind a legacy of mostly beautiful jewelry and accessories. And Ray Calish is finally Miss Ray Calish, thanks to Nancy Dearing Rossbacher.

To view an extensive collection of Calvaire jewelry and accessories, visit Jim Katz's website where he has gathered photographs from collectors all over the United States to showcase the amazing variety of this great company. Follow the link http://www.jewelrypatents.com/Calvaire/. Jim very kindly allowed me to use some of the photographs from his web pages of the Calvaire jewelry he personally owned over the years. All of it has been sold, so there is no way to obtain measurements, unfortunately. However, this gives the reader a wonderful opportunity to see a large selection of this impressive line of jewelry. Please visit his website to view an extensive collection of high end vintage costume jewelry for sale, http://www.jameskatz.com/.

Until I saw this stunning brooch, I thought I owned the most gorgeous piece of Calvaire jewelry I had ever seen. I think you will agree that this trembler brooch, with 10 beautifully enameled violets dotted with center stones and its lovely bow, is quite simply exquisite. The flowers and the leaves are wired on, allowing the trembling, and it measures a remarkable 4" long and 3" wide, while also being an inch deep from the side view. It is signed Calvaire on a plaque and it has a three-part pin assembly. Astonishing. **$450.00 – 500.00.** Dinah Taylor collection

Reverse view of brooch.

Divine Calvaire beaded purse, marked "Made in France for Calvaire of New York," **$150.00 – 250.00.** Laney Ortega collection

Calvaire

This Calvaire blue bracelet is a rare find, it also came in red, it has large unfoiled glass stones each mounted on its own link, and it has a safety chain. It is marked "Calvaire" and "Sterling." Bracelet is 7½" long and ¾" wide, the blue stones are 1" long, gold wash over sterling, $500.00 – 600.00. Author collection

This was sold to me as a jewelry pouch, it has a tag inside reading "Made in France Especially for Calvaire New York," and the golden ring is attached with a cord strap, it loops over and opens to allow you to place items inside. Pouch is 3" wide by 3⅜" tall, and is the only one I have ever seen, $75.00 – 85.00. Author collection

View of pouch opened.

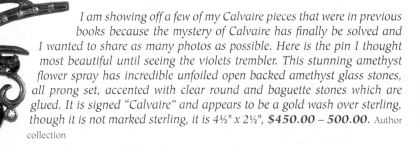

I am showing off a few of my Calvaire pieces that were in previous books because the mystery of Calvaire has finally be solved and I wanted to share as many photos as possible. Here is the pin I thought most beautiful until seeing the violets trembler. This stunning amethyst flower spray has incredible unfoiled open backed amethyst glass stones, all prong set, accented with clear round and baguette stones which are glued. It is signed "Calvaire" and appears to be a gold wash over sterling, though it is not marked sterling, it is 4½" x 2½", **$450.00 – 500.00.** Author collection

Golden flower by pin by Calvaire, with clear rhinestone accents, very heavy and dimensional, 2⅝" x 2¼" and 1⅜" in depth, signed "Calvaire," **$125.00 – 150.00.** Author collection

Beautiful amethyst flower pin with clear baguettes placed sideways in the stem, signed "Calvaire," 2½" x 1⅝", **$250.00 – 295.00.** Author collection

Topaz flower pin by Calvaire with large round prong-set topaz glass stones, and square topaz stones in stem, 2½" x 1⅝", round stones are unfoiled and open backed, **$175.00 – 195.00.** Author collection

Calvaire

This is the Calvaire debutante in a fur clip, she is signed "Calvaire," and has green rhinestones, **$350.00 – 450.00.** James Katz archive collection/Photo courtesy of James Katz

Reverse view of clip, see signature on her arm.

*Blackamoor opera singer came with a variety of dress pantaloon center stone colors, she is also a fur clip, 1²/₃" x 2¼", **$425.00 – 450.00.*** James Katz archive collection/Photo courtesy of James Katz

Reverse view showing signature on top of clip.

Reverse view of pins showing marks.

*Edwardian lady and gentleman wearing hats, both are signed "Calvaire" and "Sterling" and are pins, **$395.00 – 495.00** for matched pair.* James Katz archive collection/Photo courtesy of James Katz

Harlequin head pin from 1943 in sterling with black mask enamel and rhinestone hat, signed "Calvaire" and "Sterling," 1½" x 1", **$125.00 – 175.00.** James Katz archive collection/ Photo courtesy of James Katz

Reverse view of pin.

Matching Harlequin pin with enameled black mask, rhinestone hat, and tie of imitation pearls, signed "Calvaire," and "Sterling" twice, fur clip is 1½" x 1", **$125.00 – 175.00.** James Katz archive collection/Photo courtesy of James Katz

Fabulous little galloping horse with turquoise cabochons across middle, signed "Calvaire," **$195.00 – 255.00.** James Katz archive collection/Photo courtesy of James Katz

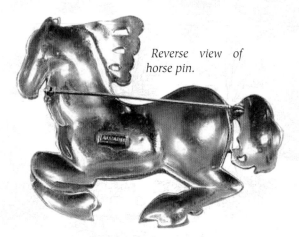

Reverse view of horse pin.

Little lamb with pavéd body of rhinestones and red cabochons with enameled green leaf collar and black ears, signed "Calvaire" and "Sterling," 1¼" x 1¾", **$395.00 – 495.00.** James Katz archive collection/Photo courtesy of James Katz

Reverse view of lamb.

Patriotic eagle with red and blue baguettes and a clear rhinestone body, with tiny blue stone eye, **$350.00 – 450.00.** James Katz archive collection/Photo courtesy of James Katz

Reverse view of pin.

Swirled ribbon pin with clear rhinestones and red cabochons, signed "Calvaire," red cabochons are open backed, **$395.00 – 495.00.** James Katz archive collection/Photo courtesy of James Katz

Swirl pin with unfoiled open back green glass stones, square green stones, and clear rhinestones, signed "Sterling Calvaire," **$225.00 – 275.00.** James Katz archive collection/Photo courtesy of James Katz

Reverse view of pin.

40

Calvaire in amber and amethyst, two colors which frequently show up in Calvaire jewelry, this one has a large amber cabochon surrounded by square amethyst glass stones, and signed "Calvaire," 1¾" in diameter, **$150.00 – 195.00.** James Katz archive collection/Photo courtesy of James Katz

Reverse view showing mark.

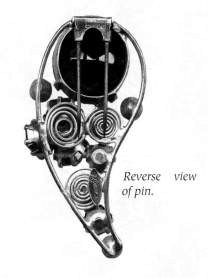

Reverse view of pin.

This is a well known pin design made for a great variety of companies and with a great variety of stone shapes and color combinations. This Calvaire version is a fur clip with aqua, clear, and amethyst stones, **$195.00 – 295.00.** James Katz archive collection/Photo courtesy of James Katz

This looks like a stylized bug to me, with a large red glass stone body, signed "Calvaire," **$150.00 – 250.00.** James Katz archive collection/Photo courtesy of James Katz

Pale blue and medium blue flower pin by Calvaire with large round prong set pale blue and medium blue glass stones, and square pale blue stones in stem, 2½" x 1⅝", round stones are unfoiled and open backed, **$175.00 – 195.00.** James Katz archive collection/Photo courtesy of James Katz

Emerald green and clear rhinestone fur clip with two blue cabochons on either side of the bottom, signed "Calvaire Sterling," **$195.00 – 295.00.** James Katz archive collection/Photo courtesy of James Katz

Reverse view of fur clip.

Side view of fur clip.

"Calvaire Sterling" key to my heart pin with a red cabochon heart dangling from the key, **$150.00 – 195.00.** James Katz archive collection/Photo courtesy of James Katz

View of signature marks.

Reverse view of pin,

Gold wash over sterling flower pin with amber center stone, signed *"Calvaire Sterling,"* **$150.00 – 195.00.** James Katz archive collection/Photo courtesy of James Katz

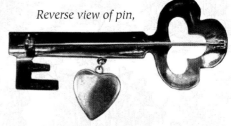

Signature on back of pin.

Reverse view of pin.

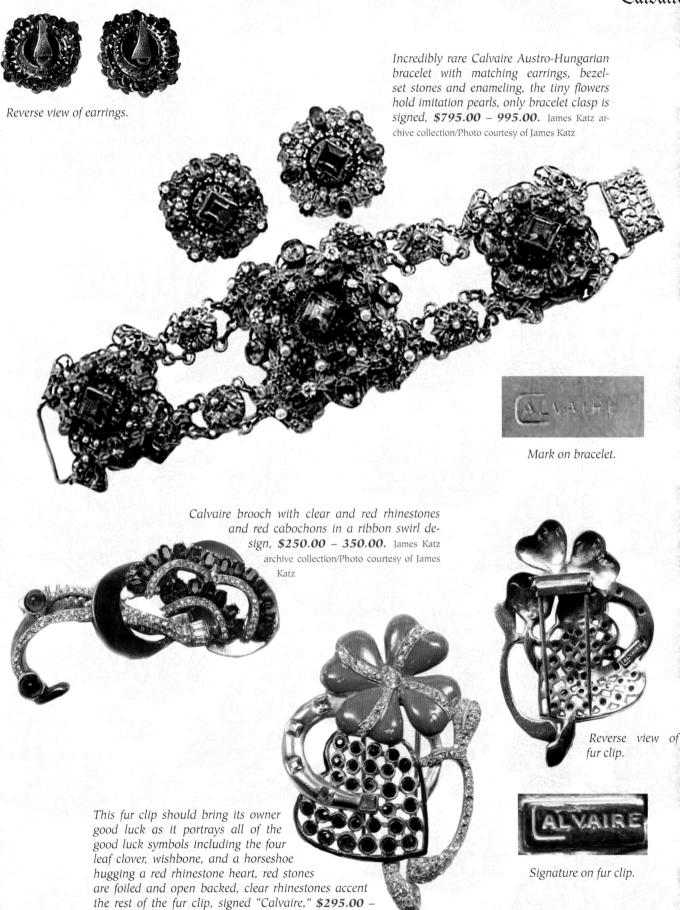

Reverse view of earrings.

Incredibly rare Calvaire Austro-Hungarian bracelet with matching earrings, bezel-set stones and enameling, the tiny flowers hold imitation pearls, only bracelet clasp is signed, **$795.00 – 995.00.** James Katz archive collection/Photo courtesy of James Katz

Mark on bracelet.

Calvaire brooch with clear and red rhinestones and red cabochons in a ribbon swirl design, **$250.00 – 350.00.** James Katz archive collection/Photo courtesy of James Katz

Reverse view of fur clip.

This fur clip should bring its owner good luck as it portrays all of the good luck symbols including the four leaf clover, wishbone, and a horseshoe hugging a red rhinestone heart, red stones are foiled and open backed, clear rhinestones accent the rest of the fur clip, signed "Calvaire," **$295.00 – 395.00.** James Katz archive collection/Photo courtesy of James Katz

Signature on fur clip.

Calvaire

Reverse view of pin.

*Calvaire leaf pin accented with prong-set red rhinestones, gold wash over sterling, marked "Calvaire" and "Sterling," **$150.00 – 195.00.** James Katz archive collection/Photo courtesy of James Katz*

Reverse view of pin.

*Calvaire lantern pin, signed, I have actually seen this design with different signatures on the back, **$125.00 – 175.00.** James Katz archive collection/Photo courtesy of James Katz*

*Calvaire black beaded hand bag, with a tag inside reading "Made in France Especially for Calvaire New York," tiny clasp has black and gold beads hand wired on, top of frame has large black glass beads and small black and gold beads wired on in a woven pattern, and the handle has four rows of gold and black beads. Bag is 6½" x 5½", in great condition, **$165.00 – 265.00.** Author collection*

Patriotic Jewelry

Each year on the fourth of July, collectors of vintage costume jewelry root through their jewelry boxes and pull out their flag pins to celebrate Independence Day. But patriotic jewelry is more than just flag jewelry, and there are a surprising number of holidays to wear your patriotic jewelry. Nearly every month of the year has one day celebrating a form of patriotism.

In January we celebrate Martin Luther King, Jr's birthday; February is President's Day; Arbor Day is in April; and May sees two days of celebration with Armed Forces Day and Memorial Day. Flag Day comes in the middle of June and of course Independence Day is July fourth. That's it until September, which has Patriot Day, Labor Day, Citizenship Day, and Constitution Day. October has Columbus Day, while November sees Election Day and Veteran's Day. December celebrates with National Pearl Harbor Remembrance Day and Bill of Rights Day. And every fourth year you can add Inauguration Day in January.

And you don't have to have a flag pin to celebrate. Many companies made patriotic jewelry in the form of eagles and torches. One of the most famous torches is the Startet torch pin featuring a lovely manicured hand holding aloft a flaming torch. The original Staret torch can sell for up to $1,600.00 but you can find a great reproduction for less than $300.00, and a cheap imitation for less than $30.00. Boucher and DeRosa also designed brooches depicting hands holding torches.

Nearly every company made some type of patriotic or regal jewelry, including Coro, Monet, Napier, Weiss, Danecraft, Marvella, Ledo, Ciner, Accessocraft, Boucher, Sarah Coventry, and even Avon. Silson made a great variety of patriotic pins and Nettie Rosenstein and Reja specialized in regal patriotic jewelry. But the most prolific make of patriotic and regal jewelry is Trifari. They not only made flag pins and eagle pins, but Uncle Sam's hat; V's for victory; red, white, and blue ribbons and bows; and airplanes. Trifari also honored the Armed Forces with insignia pins. They even designed pins that were not patriotic, such as flower bouquets but they designed them in red, white, and blue to allow them to be worn as patriotic tributes.

And since World War ll began in 1941, during the most prolific times for costume jewelry manufacture in the United States, you can find patriotic jewelry in every medium from rhinestone encrusted sterling to Bakelite to carved wooden pins.

But patriotic pins are not limited to flags and eagles. You can find red, white, and blue Christmas tree pins, such as those designed by Larry Vrba, Christopher Radko, and the LIA Company. And many collectors simply wear any jewelry that has the three colors as patriotic jewelry. Expert collector Davida Baron states it simply, "I believe that patriotic jewelry goes beyond wearing the American flag, the American eagle, or jewelry that depicts the time of war. Vintage brooches and necklaces that include the colors of old Glory … red, white, and blue, show the individuality of one's pride in our country."

No one will doubt your patriotism when they see you coming wearing this gaily waving flag by Candace Loheed of Ruby Z. This red, white, and blue creation has bold bright beads and the flag centerpiece is 3½" x 2½", necklace is 19" long, **$165.00 – 195.00.** Author collection

Patriotic Jewelry

This lovely brooch is perfect to wear for patriotic times, it has a large red glass heart surrounded by red and blue glass stones, the bottom heart dangles from the top of the brooch. This 1930s brooch is unsigned but definitely looks like a designer piece and possibly a one of a kind design. This pot metal brooch is 3" x 2¼", **$350.00 – 395.00.** Davida Baron collection/Photo courtesy of Davida Baron

Ian St. Gielar red, white, and blue patriotic designed set with necklace, bracelet, and matching earrings, all pieces are signed. Necklace has vintage red, white, and blue glass beads leading down to three triangular segments with vintage white glass flowers embedded with hand-sewn red and blue glass seed beads. Note the center of each segment has a star design, bracelet has same design as do clip earrings. Necklace is 16" with a 5" extender, bracelet is 8" x 2¼" long and earrings are 1½" x 1½", one is signed Stanley Hagler and the other is signed Ian St. Gielar. **$695.00 – 795.00.** Davida Baron collection/Photo courtesy of Davida Baron

Reverse view of set.

46

This is a most fabulous 1930s American flag brooch with rich red and clear prong-set stones, and 48 tiny blue stones, brooch is 2½" x 3", note two chains dangling with red glass beads attached, **$175.00 – 225.00.** Davida Baron collection/ Photo courtesy of Davida Baron

Reverse view showing all stones are open backed.

Unsigned Hattie Carnegie red, clear, and blue necklace, other pieces in the set were signed, this necklace is perfect to wear for patriotic holidays. Corn flower blue poured glass stones and ruby red cabochons are accented with clear rhinestones, necklace is 14" long, **$165.00 – 195.00.** Davida Baron collection/Photo courtesy of Davida Baron

Reverse view of necklace.

Patriotic Jewelry

Patriotic dress clip in red, clear, and blue prong-set rhinestones, unsigned, 3" x 2½", $150.00 – 165.00. Davida Baron collection/Photo courtesy of Davida Baron

This duette is something you rarely see, a design by Joseph Weisner NY and signed as such. This red, clear, and blue duette is perfect for holiday wear. Stones around the outer rim are foiled and open backed, 3" x 2⅛", $350.00 – 395.00. Davida Baron collection/Photo courtesy of Davida Baron

Reverse view of duette.

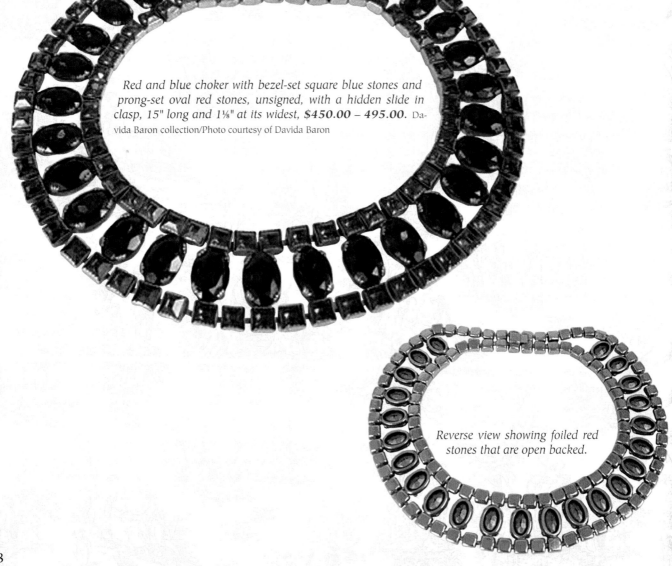

Red and blue choker with bezel-set square blue stones and prong-set oval red stones, unsigned, with a hidden slide in clasp, 15" long and 1⅛" at its widest, $450.00 – 495.00. Davida Baron collection/Photo courtesy of Davida Baron

Reverse view showing foiled red stones that are open backed.

Artful Plastics

Hattie Carnegie white and pink brooch made of wood and plastic, probably a WW2 design. The swirly pink pieces are wood, **$125.00 – 165.00**. Robin Valiunas collection

Reverse view of pin.

This collection of the same design and style horse heads came in cherry juice Bakelite, Lucite and wood. Bakelite horse, **$375.00 – 395.00**; Lucite horse, **$75.00 – 95.00**; and wooden horse, **$45.00 – 55.00**. Dinah Taylor collection

Pair of matched scarf brooches, one in Bakelite and the other in wood. Bakelite hinged scarf holder brooch, 4", **$275.00 – 295.00**. Wood carved hinged scarf holder brooch, 4", **$125.00 – 150.00**. Dinah Taylor collection

Side view showing depth of brooch.

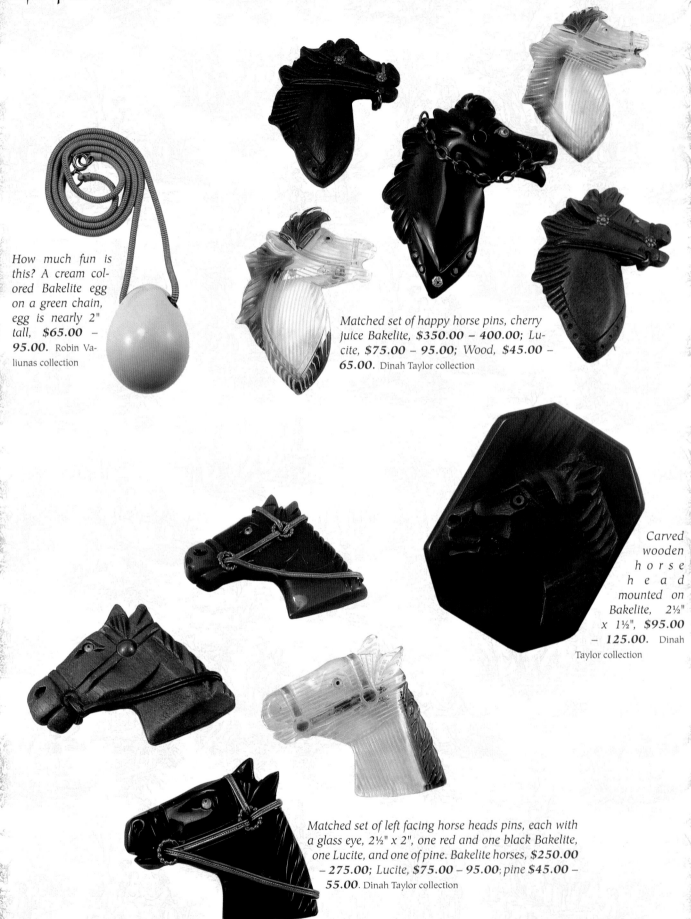

How much fun is this? A cream colored Bakelite egg on a green chain, egg is nearly 2" tall, **$65.00 – 95.00.** Robin Valiunas collection

Matched set of happy horse pins, cherry juice Bakelite, **$350.00 – 400.00;** *Lucite,* **$75.00 – 95.00;** *Wood,* **$45.00 – 65.00.** Dinah Taylor collection

Carved wooden horse head mounted on Bakelite, 2½" x 1½", **$95.00 – 125.00.** Dinah Taylor collection

Matched set of left facing horse heads pins, each with a glass eye, 2½" x 2", one red and one black Bakelite, one Lucite, and one of pine. Bakelite horses, **$250.00 – 275.00;** *Lucite,* **$75.00 – 95.00;** *pine* **$45.00 – 55.00.** Dinah Taylor collection

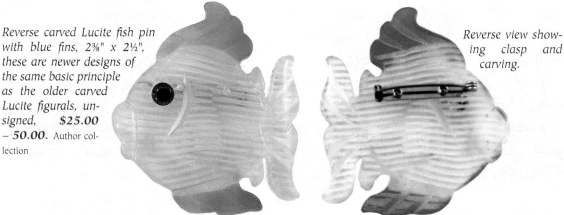

Reverse carved Lucite fish pin with blue fins, 2⅜" x 2½", these are newer designs of the same basic principle as the older carved Lucite figurals, unsigned, **$25.00 – 50.00.** Author collection

Reverse view showing clasp and carving.

Reverse carved Lucite lobster with blue fins, 4" long, unsigned, another newer design, **$25.00 – 50.00.** Author collection

Reverse carved Lucite horse head pin, though newer designs, these are still quite fun to collect and wear, horse head is 3½" x 3", and over ¼" thick, and very heavy for its size, **$30.00 – 55.00.** Author collection

Pair of sailors in plastic with hand painting, rhinestones, and pearl heads, 2⅜" x 2", unsigned, **$75.00 – 95.00.** Author collection

Wonderful Bakelite carved oranges dangling from sliced log pin, in excellent condition, oranges are very large, ¾" or 21 mm, pin dangles to 2½", with five oranges, **$255.00 – 295.00.** Author collection

Vegetable garden Bakelite pin with a bell pepper, a turnip, and a tomato, each with paint accents, 2" x 2", $395.00 – 425.00. Author collection

Pair of berries Bakelite fruit pin with two red carved fruits, 2⅛" x 1⅝", $375.00 – 395.00. Author collection

Bakelite bananas pin with bananas dangling from a large green carved leaf, 3⅛" x 3¼", $225.00 – 295.00. Author collection

Bakelite carved red bow pin with dangling red berries, 3¼" x 2½", $325.00 – 395.00. Author collection

Fabulous carved burgundy Bakelite plum pin, 2¼" x 1½", stem is painted plastic, $295.00 – 350.00. Author collection

Reverse view of Bakelite plum.

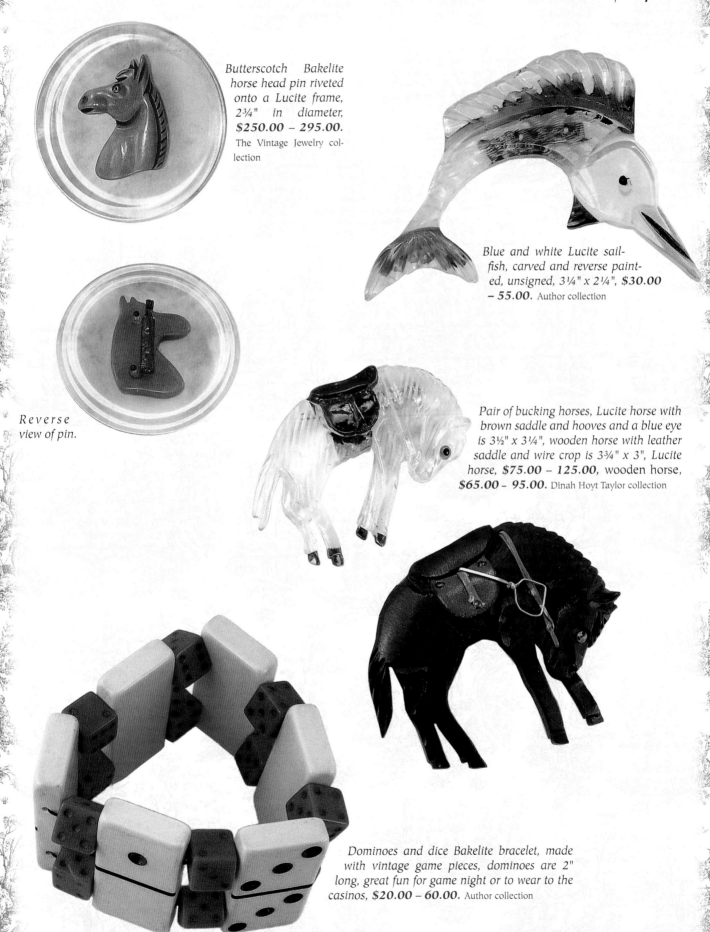

Butterscotch Bakelite horse head pin riveted onto a Lucite frame, 2¾" in diameter, **$250.00 – 295.00**. The Vintage Jewelry collection

Blue and white Lucite sailfish, carved and reverse painted, unsigned, 3¼" x 2¼", **$30.00 – 55.00.** Author collection

Reverse view of pin.

Pair of bucking horses, Lucite horse with brown saddle and hooves and a blue eye is 3½" x 3¼", wooden horse with leather saddle and wire crop is 3¾" x 3", Lucite horse, **$75.00 – 125.00**, wooden horse, **$65.00 – 95.00.** Dinah Hoyt Taylor collection

Dominoes and dice Bakelite bracelet, made with vintage game pieces, dominoes are 2" long, great fun for game night or to wear to the casinos, **$20.00 – 60.00.** Author collection

Quality

Sensational Eisenberg Original brooch with bright green stones, 2¾" x 4¼", brooch is marked only "Eisenberg" but it appeared in an ad in February 1941 for Eisenberg Originals, **$695.00 – 995.00.** Cynthia Fore Miller collection

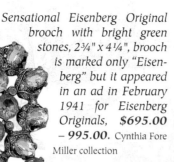

Eisenberg Original fur clip with wonderful variety of clear rhinestones is exquisite in person, measuring 2¾" x 1½", **$195.00 – 295.00.** Laney Ortega collection

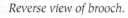

Reverse view of brooch.

Reverse view of fur clip.

Rare and magnificent Eisenberg sterling set of ring with matching earrings in emerald shaped rhinestones, **$450.00 – 850.00.** Laney Ortega collection

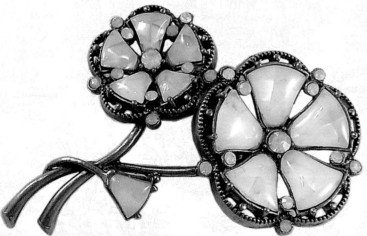

Hollycraft opaline flower pin is quite an unusual find, 2¼", the opalescent glass stones are shaped like bells, including the one leaf, **$110.00 – 145.00.** Frances E. (Jean) Mitchell collection

Delightful Coro Calopsitta birds duette in silver-tone pot metal, it is convertible to a pair of matching fur clips. These cockatoos are enameled in pink and blue with black highlights, red eyes, and pavé rhinestone heads. This 3⅝" x 2⅛" duette brooch is in excellent condition with nearly perfect enameling, the design patent for this set is 126,490 dated 1941. This is also a fairly rare version of this famous duette, since they usually feature pavé bodies or wings instead of a pavé head, **$165.00 – 225.00.** Mary Ann Docktor-Smith collection

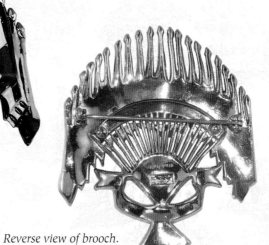

Reverse view showing duette mechanism.

Well known Coro Siempre Amigos brooch featuring enameled flags on individual flagpoles and draped with a ribbon stating in Spanish, "Friends forever." It is marked "Coro" and "Pat. No. 130,836," which was issued to Lester Gaba, a designer for Cohn & Rosenberger in December 1941. The brooch was designed to commemorate a 1938 conference held in Lima, Peru, with North and South American nations joining to discourse on the war in Europe. It measures 2⅝" x 2⅜", **$300.00 – 325.00.** Mary Ann Docktor-Smith collection

Reverse view of brooch.

Eugene black flower pin is heavily japanned and features hand-wired glass beads and crystals, with delicate flower and leaf detailing, 2" in diameter and signed "Eugene" in script, **$135.00 – 155.00.** Mary Ann Docktor-Smith collection

Reverse view of brooch.

Enchanting little DeMario turtle pin with pavé rhinestone head, green eyes, and a shell back of hand-wired rhinestone headpins, green glass beads, and baroque faux pearls, 2½" x 1¼" and signed "DeMario" in script, **$125.00 – 150.00.** Mary Ann Docktor-Smith collection

Reverse view of pin showing signature cartouche.

Outstanding pair of snake clip earrings with large dark green cabochon centers accented with genuine looking stones, these 1" x 1⅜" earrings are not signed but are an exact design match to marked Selro pieces of jewelry, **$80.00 – 115.00.** Mary Ann Docktor-Smith collection

*This dazzling green floral vase pin has very high quality faceted crystal flowers atop a faceted green glass vase; it is unsigned and 2⅞" x 1¼", **$375.00 – 395.00.*** Jayne Spencer collection

*Spectacular double mushroom fur clip with aurora borealis stones in amber and topaz, and underneath the mushrooms you will find a row of pink baguettes. This clip is substantial and weighty, 2¾" x 1⅞" and excellent quality, though unsigned, **$275.00 – 300.00.*** Jayne Spencer collection

Reverse view of pin.

Reverse view of fur clip.

Reverse view of pin.

Marcel Boucher resplendent bird brooch, I believe this is the quetzal, a bird found only in Central America. Brooch is 4" x 1⅝" and has the Phrygian Cap mark of Boucher. His enameling is worn, so value reflects his condition up to an excellent condition, **$475.00 – 775.00.** Jayne Spencer collection

This Trifari swooping bird brooch comes with a variety of stone color combinations, he is signed "Trifari" and has a patent of 142,659 dated June 27, 1945. Note rhinestone accents sprinkled on his tail like salt, 3" x 2", **$375.00 – 450.00.** Jayne Spencer collection

Reverse view of brooch.

Unsigned De Rosa floral brooch with three blossoms bearing light sapphire stamens and clear rhinestone leaf accents, 3⅞" x 2½", a very beautiful and classic design, **$295.00 – 350.00.** Jayne Spencer collection

Reverse view of brooch.

Quality

Mazer gold-plated flower brooch with sapphire colored center stone and accented with rhinestones, 2" in diameter, **$295.00 – 395.00.** Cheryl Killmer collection

Marvelous Hattie Carnegie elephant and howdah brooch, with lovely imitation jade and pearl accents, notice the bracelets around the elephants legs, 2½" x 2, **$395.00 – 495.00.** Cheryl Killmer collection

Enameled Ciner clip panther earrings in black with green cabochon eyes, holding a pavé rhinestone ring, 1½", **$95.00 – 150.00.** Cheryl Killmer collection

Miriam Haskell double strand gray baroque pearl necklace, with hand-beaded clasp, **$225.00 – 425.00.** Cheryl Killmer collection

Lovely Coro pink moonglow cabochon brooch in a double feather design, accented with clear rhinestones, **$200.00 – 250.00.** Cheryl Killmer

Reverse view of brooch.

This stylish enameleld link necklace is attributed to German jewelry designer Jakob Bengel, who never signed his work and whose designs spanned the 1920s and 1930s Art Deco period, **$200.00 – 300.00.** Cheryl Killmer collection

Another enameled link necklace attributed to Jakob Bengel, **$200.00 – 300.00.** Cheryl Killmer collection

ART African Masks parure, gunmetal with imitation semi precious cabs. Necklace 20" chain, pendent 2⅝" x 2", bracelet 6¾" x 1", brooch 2⅝" x 2", earrings 1¼" x 1⅛", **$550.00 – 750.00.** Cheryl Killmer collection

View showing signature.

Reverse view of brooch.

*Valentino silver-tone lavender and purple orchid brooch with push pin clasp on top for extra support, 5" x 4", **$595.00 – 700.00.** Cheryl Killmer collection*

*Dog collar necklace and earrings with 1⁵⁄₁₆" unfoiled emerald green glass cushion cut stones and clears, necklace 14½" x 1⅝", earrings 2¾" x ⅞", **$275.00 – 325.00.** Cheryl Killmer collection*

*Miriam Haskell starfish pin with tubular beads, purple beads, round beads, and roses montees, 3" x 3", **$150.00 – 195.00.** Cheryl Killmer collection*

Weiss huge bib of silver tone with clear navettes, pears, and dentelles, impressed "WEISS" in block letters mark, 15½" x 3¼", **$550.00 – 650.00.** Cheryl Killmer collection

Reverse view of necklace.

Mazer rhodium-plated cascading flower brooch with clear rhinestones, with hook at the bottom of the anchor, 6½" x 1⅛", **$225.00 – 250.00.** Cheryl Killmer collection

Reverse view of brooch.

Trifari Alfred Phillipe "Boise de Boulogue" fruit salad festoon/bib of white and green flowers and buds, 16" x 2¼", **$825.00 – 1,250.00.** Cheryl Killmer collection

Hattie Carnegie Asian deity pendant necklace, 20" long, pendant 4½" x 3", **$325.00 – 375.00.** Cheryl Killmer collection

Side view showing depth of bracelet.

KJL gold-tone and imitation jade and pearl dragon bracelet, 2" diameter, $450.00 – 495.00. Cheryl Killmer collection

Trifari brushed gold-tone parure with flawed emeralds and pink-ruby cabochons, necklace has extra link, bracelet 7", doorknocker earrings 2" long, button earrings 1" diameter, snake brooch 2⅞" x 1⅝", $1,500.00 – 2,000.00. Cheryl Killmer collection

Huge unsigned Hobé clip with topaz, clear, yellow, green, and pink unfoiled rhinestones, this clip was verified by Don Hobé, **$325.00 – 350.00.** Cheryl Killmer collection

Reverse view of clip.

Miriam Haskell bar pin from the 1930s, wired pearl and bezel set clear rhinestones, and rose montees in brass flowers on a brass pin frame, with curved end and groove center for the pin stem, 3½" x ¾", **$175.00 – 195.00.** Dinah Taylor collection

Reverse view of pin.

Miriam Haskell coral beads with pavé-set rhinestone leaves from the 1940s, 2½" x 1½", with a c-clasp and pierced back, **$150.00 – 175.00.** Dinah Taylor collection

Reverse view of pin.

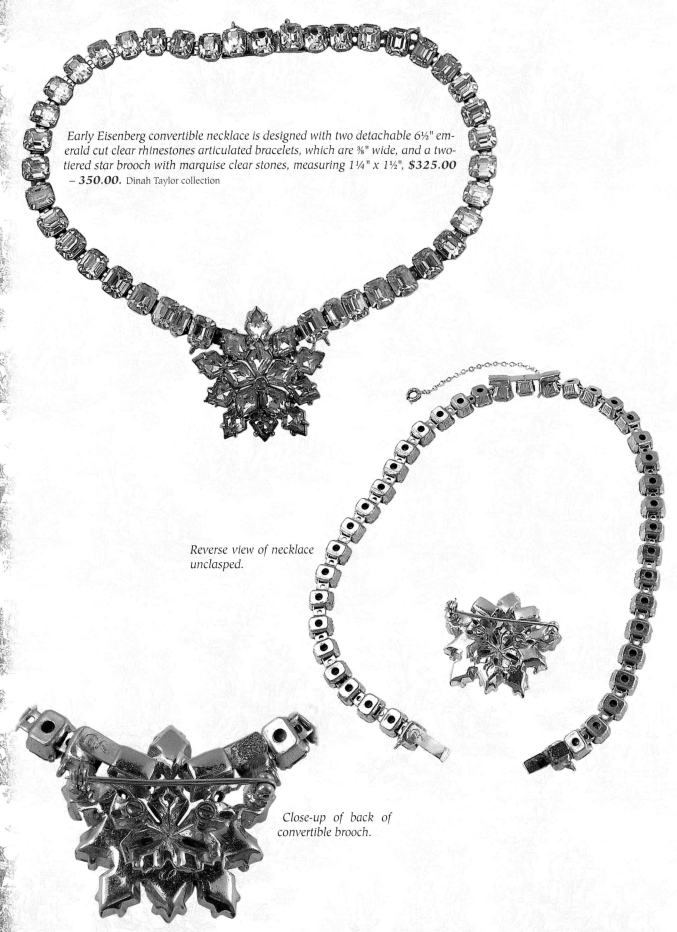

*Early Eisenberg convertible necklace is designed with two detachable 6½" emerald cut clear rhinestones articulated bracelets, which are ⅜" wide, and a two-tiered star brooch with marquise clear stones, measuring 1¼" x 1½", **$325.00 – 350.00.*** Dinah Taylor collection

Reverse view of necklace unclasped.

Close-up of back of convertible brooch.

Close-up view
of mark.

Parure by Alfred Villasana, conjoined incised "AV" mark, all pieces are marked. Necklace is 15½", bracelet 7", and earrings are ⅞" x ¾". Alfredo Villasana worked for William Spratling at one time, **$1,200.00 – 1,300.00.**
Dinah Taylor collection

Here is a beautiful Ralph de Rosa Sterling fur clip with unusual cut aquamarine open backed, large unfoiled stone, and ruby red emerald-cut unfoiled and clear rhinestones, 2¾" x 3", marked "R DE ROSA STERLING," **$225.00 – 250.00.** Kay Heino collection

Here is the enormous Trifari Alfred Phillipe designed clear Lucite jelly belly fur clip from 1943, gold vermeil over sterling, clear pavé set rhinestones, red glass bullet cabochon eye, Des.Pat. No. 135,177. Marked "Trifari STERLING," **$275.00 – 300.00.**
Kay Heino collection

Reverse view of fur clip.

Reverse view of fur clip.

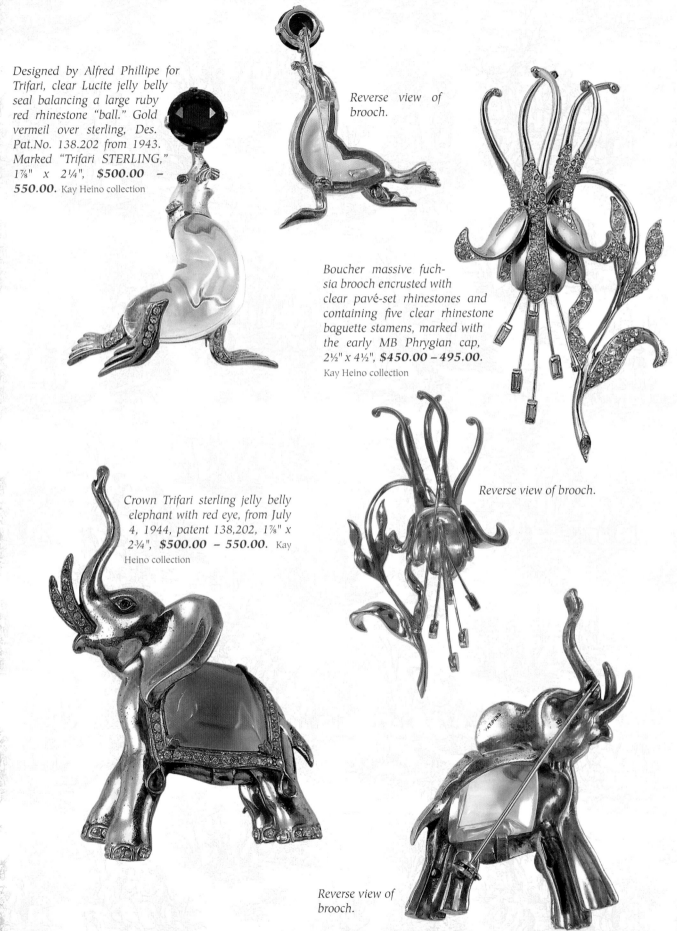

Designed by Alfred Phillipe for Trifari, clear Lucite jelly belly seal balancing a large ruby red rhinestone "ball." Gold vermeil over sterling, Des. Pat.No. 138.202 from 1943. Marked "Trifari STERLING," 1⅞" x 2¼", **$500.00 – 550.00.** Kay Heino collection

Reverse view of brooch.

Boucher massive fuchsia brooch encrusted with clear pavé-set rhinestones and containing five clear rhinestone baguette stamens, marked with the early MB Phrygian cap, 2½" x 4½", **$450.00 – 495.00.** Kay Heino collection

Crown Trifari sterling jelly belly elephant with red eye, from July 4, 1944, patent 138,202, 1⅞" x 2¾", **$500.00 – 550.00.** Kay Heino collection

Reverse view of brooch.

Reverse view of brooch.

Eisenberg sterling fur clip, enormous, heavy 1940s sterling fur clip with clear rhinestones and ruby red chaton, oval teardrop, and marquise cut rhinestones, marked "EISENBERG STERLING," 2¼" x 3¼", **$275.00 – 300.00.** Kay Heino collection

Reverse view of fur clip.

Eisenberg sterling fur clip, beautiful 1940s fur clip with unusual cut amethyst and rose colored unfoiled glass stones and small clear rhinestones, gold vermeil over sterling, marked "EISENBERG STERLING," 2¼" x 3", **$250.00 – 300.00.**

Kay Heino collection

Reverse view of fur clip.

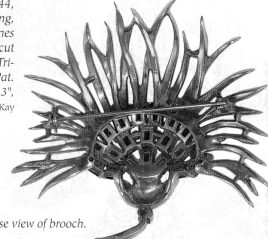

Trifari sterling chrysanthemum brooch, well known Alfred Phillipe designed brooch from 1944, gold vermeil over sterling, clear pavé-set rhinestones and ruby red emerald-cut rhinestones, marked "Trifari STERLING, Des.Pat. No. 137,543," 3" x 3", **$400.00 – 425.00.** Kay Heino collection

Reverse view of brooch.

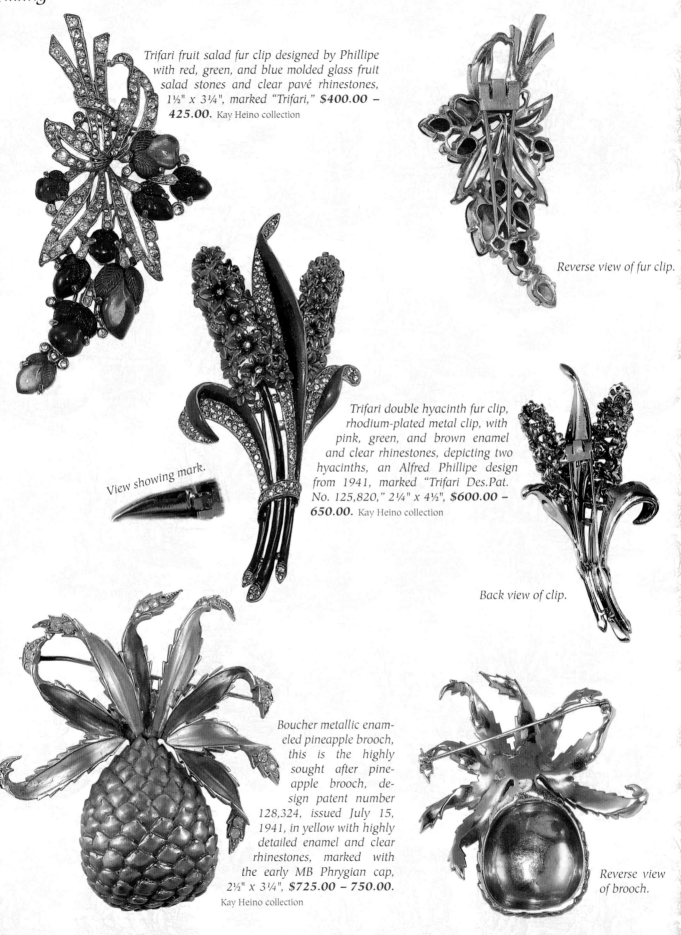

Trifari fruit salad fur clip designed by Phillipe with red, green, and blue molded glass fruit salad stones and clear pavé rhinestones, 1½" x 3¼", marked "Trifari," **$400.00 – 425.00.** Kay Heino collection

Reverse view of fur clip.

View showing mark.

Trifari double hyacinth fur clip, rhodium-plated metal clip, with pink, green, and brown enamel and clear rhinestones, depicting two hyacinths, an Alfred Phillipe design from 1941, marked "Trifari Des.Pat. No. 125,820," 2¼" x 4½", **$600.00 – 650.00.** Kay Heino collection

Back view of clip.

Boucher metallic enameled pineapple brooch, this is the highly sought after pineapple brooch, design patent number 128,324, issued July 15, 1941, in yellow with highly detailed enamel and clear rhinestones, marked with the early MB Phrygian cap, 2½" x 3¼", **$725.00 – 750.00.** Kay Heino collection

Reverse view of brooch.

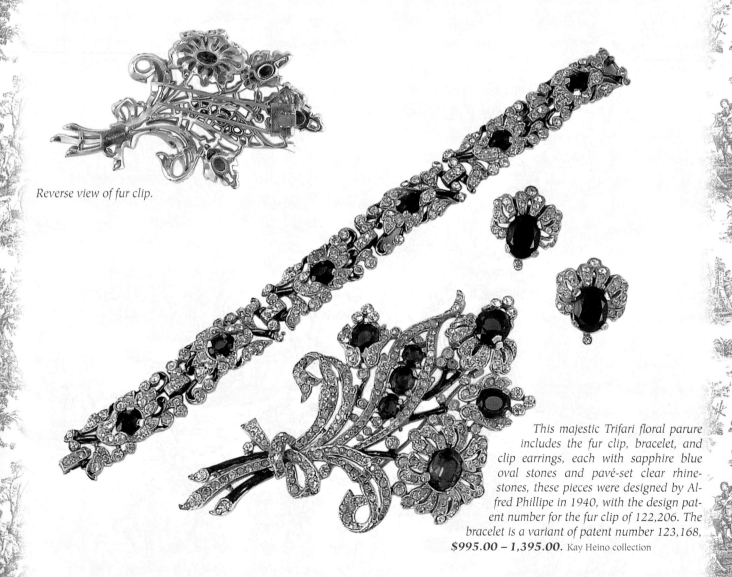

Gold vermeil-plated sterling triquette which is three fur clips in rhinestones and enamel, representing three birds perched on branches, each fur clip is marked "Sterling," the frame is marked "Coro Duette STER-LING" with "Des.Pat.No. 133,478," **$200.00 – 250.00.**
Kay Heino collection

Reverse view of triquette.

Reverse view of fur clip.

This majestic Trifari floral parure includes the fur clip, bracelet, and clip earrings, each with sapphire blue oval stones and pavé-set clear rhinestones, these pieces were designed by Alfred Phillipe in 1940, with the design patent number for the fur clip of 122,206. The bracelet is a variant of patent number 123,168, **$995.00 – 1,395.00.** Kay Heino collection

Absolutely stunning Edlee purple parure with 15" necklace featuring a 1½" drop centerpiece, 2¼" x 1½" brooch, 7" bracelet, and 1½" x¾" earrings, $400.00 – 600.00. Lisa Boydstun collection

Histoire de Verre poured glass seven strand necklace of amethyst glass beads, 17", **$2,000.00 – 2,250.00.** Judy Miller collection

Jomaz convertible parure cobalt glass set with baguettes, necklace is 14½" but extends to 21¾", brace-let is 7½", and clip earrings are 1½", $350.00 – 375.00. Judy Miller collection

Coppola e Toppo green and blue glass necklace, 32", $2,400.00 – 2,600.00. Judy Miller collection

Coppola e Toppo green neck-lace and clip earrings set, necklace is 17" while earrings are 1", $800.00 – 900.00. Judy Miller collection

This sophisticated Tulla Booth parure is from the 1980s, with 18½" necklace, cuff bracelet, and clip earrings that are 1½", $1,200.00 – 1,300.00. Judy Miller collection

Bracelet and earrings.

William de Lillo gold-tone set with white seed
beads, necklace is 28" long and bracelet is 8" x 2¼",
$800.00 – 850.00. Judy Miller collection

Miriam Haskell necklace and earrings set,
the baskets on the chain have pearls inside,
necklace is 21½" long and clip earrings are
1¼", **$525.00 – 575.00.** Judy Miller collection

Close up of pin showing signature.

Joseff Hollywood silver leaf pin, 2½" diameter, bracelet 7¼" x ¾", screw back earrings are 1" x¾", **$450.00 – 495.00.** Sherry James collection

Reverse view of fur clip.

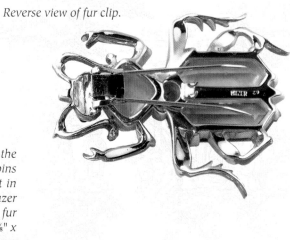

This is one of the most gorgeous pins you can ever meet in person, it is a Mazer enameled and rhinestone bug fur clip, with pavé accented legs, 2⅜" x 1⅝", **$395.00 – 495.00.** Sherry James collection

Trifari sterling vermeil deco bracelet with large aqua unfoiled stones, 7½" x 1", **$500.00 – 550.00.** Sherry James collection

Side view showing depth of bracelet and stones.

Original Deja floral brooch with enameling and rhinestones, brooch is likely from the 1930s, and is signed on the back "Original Deja" which later became Reja. Brooch is 4¼" x 2", **$175.00 – 195.00.** Davida Baron collection/Photo courtesy of Davida Baron

Reverse view of brooch.

Reverse view showing signature.

D e l i g h t f u l Hobé necklace from the late 1940s or early 1950s, with a gorgeous link chain which has an open filigree design and is enameled, separated by a bezel-set green glass stone. The pendant has a Russian gold beading design, with imitation pearls and rhinestones, accented with enameling. Necklace is 16" long and pendant is 4" x 2⅞", and signed "Hobé" on back, **$250.00 – 295.00.** Davida Baron collection/Photo courtesy of Davida Baron

This incredible corsage pin is from the 1920s, with trembling flowers with clear, pale lavender and smoky blue rhinestones, leaves are silver-colored wire with imitation pearls and clear rhinestones, brooch is 6½" by 3", **$400.00 – 450.00.** Davida Baron collection/Photo courtesy of Davida Baron

Amazingly beautiful Staret brooch with light and dark purple enamel and amethyst and clear rhinestones, signed "Staret," 5" x 2½", **$195.00 – 225.00.** Davida Baron collection/Photo courtesy of Davida Baron

Reverse view of Staret brooch.

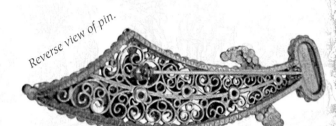

Korda "Thief of Bagdad" saber from the collection of jewelry made to promote the film, it is enameled and has rhinestones and imitation pearls. Pin is signed and is 4" x 1¼", **$175.00 – 195.00.** Davida Baron collection/Photo courtesy of Davida Baron

Reverse view of pin.

Unusual Schiaparelli necklace with ornate circular links with three topaz rhinestones on each side of each link, each circle link is 1", and necklace is signed "Schiaparelli." Necklace is 15½" long and likely from the early 1950s, **$250.00 – 295.00.** Davida Baron collection/Photo courtesy of Davida Baron

Lovely enameled brooch is not signed but appears to be the work of Boucher, note the green enameled leaves are artistically accented with red enameling. Two buds are ready to bloom and have pink enameling accented with red enameling, the center holds a gorgeous square blue topaz glass stone which is unfoiled and open backed, 3¼" x 2½", pot metal and likely from the 1940s, **$350.00 – 395.00.** Davida Baron collection/Photo courtesy of Davida Baron

View of signature on brooch.

Reverse view of brooch.

Vogue brooch from the late 1940s is a vase filled with flowers on wires that can be manipulated to make the brooch three dimensional. Brooch is covered with prong-set rhinestones, and is 2¾" x 2¼", **$250.00 – 275.00.** Davida Baron collection/Photo courtesy of Davida Baron

Eisenberg Original over-sized dress clip with amber and clear rhinestones, signed, 4" x 2⅛", **$200.00 – 295.00.** Davida Baron collection/ Photo courtesy of Davida Baron

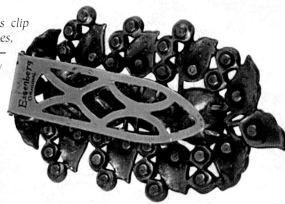

Reverse view of dress clip.

This truly magnificent brooch seems to scream Vogue, though it is unsigned, it has all of the Vogue character-istics, it appears to be an ab-stract flower-filled vase. All stones are prong set, and it has the flowers attached with wires that can be ma-nipulated to give the brooch a three-dimensional appearance, brooch is 4½" x 4", **$600.00 – 650.00.** Davida Baron collection/Photo courtesy of Davida Baron

Reverse view of brooch.

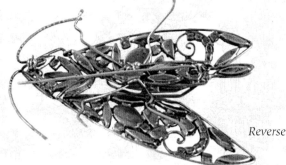

Reverse view of brooch.

Huge fly brooch constructed in two layers, enabling the wings to move. Brooch is unsigned but it has the look of an Iradj Moini design. Brooch is filled with different colors and sizes of blue stones, and the eyes are red rhinestones, 4¼" x 2½", **$700.00 – 750.00.** Davida Baron collection/Photo courtesy of Davida Baron

Regal necklace has the bold look of jewelry from the House of "de Lillo." The centerpiece with purple cabochons and clear rhinestones is 5" x 3", and the necklace is 19" long. Necklace is signed "deLillo" in the slide-in clasp, note the pearls at the end of the dangles on the centerpiece, $500.00 – 575.00. Davida Baron collection/Photo courtesy of Davida Baron

Tremendous Joseff brooch has a pair of circular cabochon-set brooches attached with chains, and accented with dangling chains and charms, signed Joseff. The circular brooches measure 1¾" each, with 5½" of connecting chains, and the dangling chains add another 4", $350.00 – 400.00. Davida Baron collection/Photo courtesy of Davida Baron

Stylized floral bouquet by Reinad with clear triangular glass stones, prong set, unfoiled, and open backed, possibly 1940s, 3¾" x 2¾", $350.00 – 395.00. Davida Baron collection/Photo courtesy of Davida Baron

Awesome bib necklace by Scaasi, a clothing designer who dabbled in jewelry design who turned his jewelry line over to Kenneth Jay Lane. While Arnold Scaasi was in charge of his jewelry, he designed all of the jewelry and made all of the decisions regarding the stones and the colors. This bib necklace has huge ruby red cabochon glass stones bezel set with clear and red prong-set stones surrounding them. Necklace has a slide in clasp with a safety chain. It is 15" long with a center depth of 2¼" and is signed "Scaasi" on the back. Scassi is Isaacs backwards. $700.00 – 750.00. Davida Baron collection/Photo courtesy of Davida Baron

Divine necklace by Schiaparelli with purple cabochons surrounded by pewter colored leaves and accented with pink rhinestones. Each link is 1" wide, and necklace is signed on back. It is 15" long and the centerpiece falls 2" down, necklace is most likely from the 1950s, $250.00 – 295.00. Davida Baron collection/Photo courtesy of Davida Baron

Reverse view of brooch.

Robert Sorrell certainly knows how to design a stunning flower vase brooch. This one has a lovely blue glass vase filled with multi-colored prong-set rhinestones. Sorrell designs his jewelry with the spirit of the 1920s, 1930s, and 1940s. Signed brooch is 3½" x 2½", $300.00 – 350.00. Davida Baron collection/Photo courtesy of Davida Baron

View showing signature.

Reverse view of brooch.

Huge Coro Craft spray brooch with unfoiled open backed emerald-cut glass stones, accented with clear rhinestones, 4" x 3-¾", signed on reverse, absolutely stunning, $350.00 – 425.00. Davida Baron collection/Photo courtesy of Davida Baron

This necklace is from the 1940s when pot metal was needed for the war effort and fine fashion jewelers used sterling in their designs. This is a Ralph De Rosa necklace with clear and aqua blue rhinestones, it has a fold-over clasp which is marked "R. De-Rosa" on one side and "Sterling" on the other, necklace is 15" long with a 4¾" center-piece, **$400.00 – 450.00.** Davida Baron collection/Photo courtesy of Davida Baron

Fur clip with turquoise glass beads surrounding marquise-shaped swirled cranberry glass stones and a cranberry glass cabochon in the center, signed "Sterling" and "Eisenberg," extremely heavy and likely made during the war years, 2½" in diameter, **$300.00 – 350.00.** Davida Baron collection/Photo courtesy of Davida Baron

Staret crystal grapes cluster brooch, signed "Staret," with large round prong-set clear rhinestones, foiled and open backed, 3½" x 2¾", **$300.00 – 350.00.** Davida Baron collection/Photo courtesy of Davida Baron

Reverse view of fur clip.

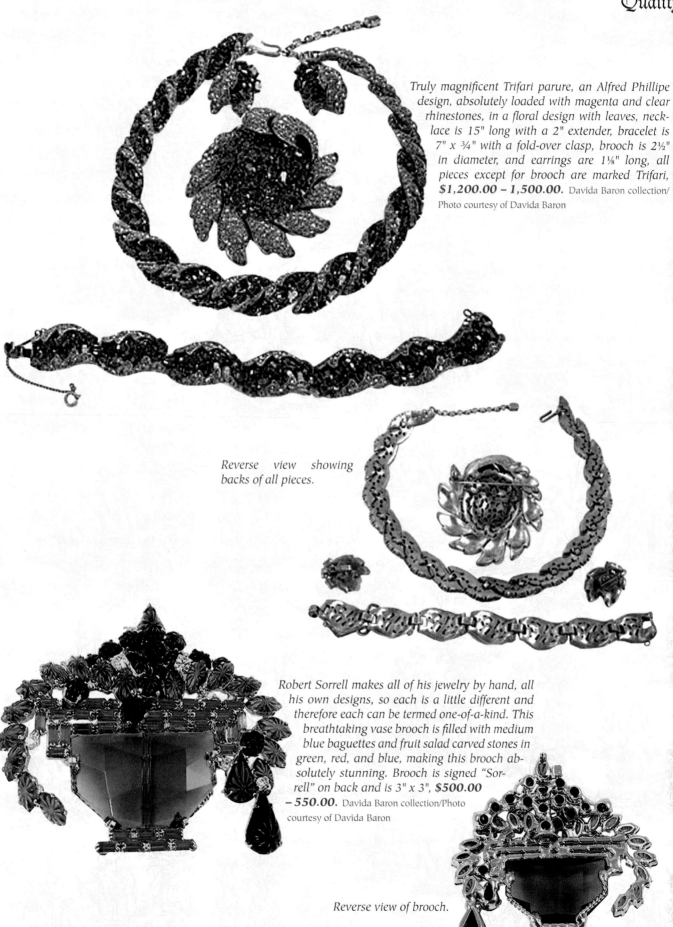

Truly magnificent Trifari parure, an Alfred Phillipe design, absolutely loaded with magenta and clear rhinestones, in a floral design with leaves, necklace is 15" long with a 2" extender, bracelet is 7" x ¾" with a fold-over clasp, brooch is 2½" in diameter, and earrings are 1⅛" long, all pieces except for brooch are marked Trifari, **$1,200.00 – 1,500.00.** Davida Baron collection/ Photo courtesy of Davida Baron

Reverse view showing backs of all pieces.

Robert Sorrell makes all of his jewelry by hand, all his own designs, so each is a little different and therefore each can be termed one-of-a-kind. This breathtaking vase brooch is filled with medium blue baguettes and fruit salad carved stones in green, red, and blue, making this brooch absolutely stunning. Brooch is signed "Sorrell" on back and is 3" x 3", **$500.00 – 550.00.** Davida Baron collection/Photo courtesy of Davida Baron

Reverse view of brooch.

Rhinestone and enameled lovebirds brooch with peach enameling, unsigned, imitation pearls suffer from flaking and brooch is in well loved condition, this is a famous Boucher design seen in many different colors in unsigned brooches and fur clips, see a pink enameled lovebirds brooch identical to this in my first book, a precious design. Brooch is 3½" wide, **$50.00 – 95.00.** Peter Tripp collection

Schiaparelli bracelet with watermelon stones surrounded by clear rhinestones, 7½" x 1", long, signed on back of clasp, **$650.00 – 695.00.** The Vintage Jewelry collection

Reverse view showing signature.

Gorgeous Original by Robert brooch with huge blue glass center stone surrounded by aurora borealis rhinestones in round and marquise shapes on a frame accenting the center stone, signed, 2¼" x 2", a quite spectacular example by Robert, **$75.00 – 95.00.** The Vintage Jewelry collection

Chanel snake skin bracelet in green, this is a hinged cuff bracelet with the CC logo on it, bracelet is ¼" wide, **$200.00 – 225.00.** The Vintage Jewelry collection

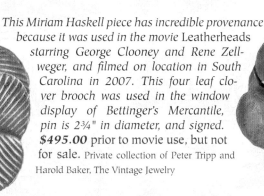

This Miriam Haskell piece has incredible provenance because it was used in the movie *Leatherheads* starring George Clooney and Rene Zell-weger, and filmed on location in South Carolina in 2007. This four leaf clo-ver brooch was used in the window display of Bettinger's Mercantile, pin is 2¾" in diameter, and signed. **$495.00** prior to movie use, but not for sale. Private collection of Peter Tripp and Harold Baker, The Vintage Jewelry

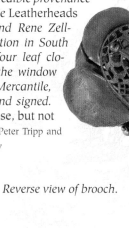

Reverse view of brooch.

Over-sized black and white pin from the House of de Lillo, signed "de Lillo" on an applied plaque, pin has black and white glass stones, all prong set, center stone has an open back, interesting to note that the white oval stones are mount-ed in a square frame, pin is nearly 3" in diameter, **$195.00 – 250.00.** Author collection

Reverse view of pin.

View of signa-ture plaque.

Fabulous root beer bracelet covered with multicolored glass stones, all bezel set, unsigned but attributed to Chanel, a 1930s design, bracelet is 1⅞" wide, **$1,500.00 – 1,600.00.** Kim Paff collection/Photo courtesy of Kim Paff, www.kimsvintage.com

I think this flower basket is one of the prettiest made by Trifari, it has green glass fruit salad stones and I have seen it with red stones also, signed "crown Trifari" and "Pat. Pend." and between the two is the num-ber "9," bottom of basket and the inside of the handle are lined with clear rhine-stones and clear stones accent the flower stones, 2¼" x 1½", **$200.00 – 225.00.** Author collection

These earrings are stunning in person, they are unsigned but an online seller of high end jewelry showed these earrings along with the marching necklace attributed to Christian Dior. Earrings have a beautiful flawed emerald glass drop, clear round and marquise prong-set stones, and tiny stones pavéd into the top of the drop holder, very well made, earrings are over 2½" long, $175.00 – 225.00. Author collection

You would have to hold this magnificent duette pin in your hands to truly appreciate it; it was made by Robert Sorrell and features two large carved flawed glass centerpiece stones, surrounded by prong-set clear rhinestones, and accented with imitation pearls. Duette pin comes apart to be worn as dress clips, signed "Sorrell Originals," I purchased this piece directly from Mr. Sorrell. Duette pin is 3½" x 1½", $325.00 – 395.00. Author collection

Reverse view showing signature clip.

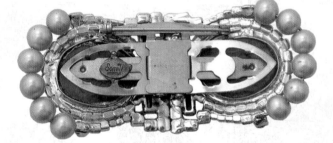

Reverse view showing mechanism.

Pins separated and shown as dress clips.

Reverse view of dress clips.

Parures & Demi Parures

Miriam Haskell set of cobalt beads with mabé pearls, necklace is 15", while screw back clip earrings are ¾", **$500.00 – 550.00.**
Judy Miller collection

Joseph Warner black rhinestone necklace with matching bracelet in silver tone, set with black marquis and chaton rhinestones and accented with clear stones. Necklace is 14¾" while bracelet is 7⅜" x 1⅛" with a push in clasp and safety chain. Both are signed "JOSEPH WARNER," **$165.00 – 195.00.** Mary Ann Docktor-Smith collection

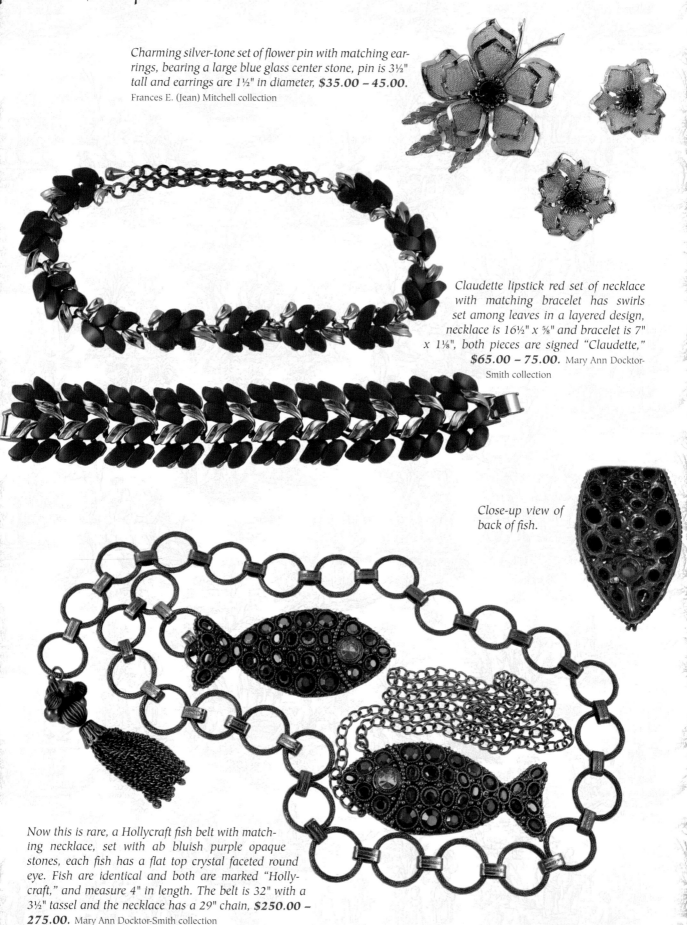

Charming silver-tone set of flower pin with matching ear-rings, bearing a large blue glass center stone, pin is 3½" tall and earrings are 1½" in diameter, **$35.00 – 45.00.**
Frances E. (Jean) Mitchell collection

Claudette lipstick red set of necklace with matching bracelet has swirls set among leaves in a layered design, necklace is 16½" x ⅝" and bracelet is 7" x 1⅛", both pieces are signed "Claudette," **$65.00 – 75.00.** Mary Ann Docktor-Smith collection

Close-up view of back of fish.

Now this is rare, a Hollycraft fish belt with match-ing necklace, set with ab bluish purple opaque stones, each fish has a flat top crystal faceted round eye. Fish are identical and both are marked "Holly-craft," and measure 4" in length. The belt is 32" with a 3½" tassel and the necklace has a 29" chain, **$250.00 – 275.00.** Mary Ann Docktor-Smith collection

Reverse view of bracelet.

This smart set in silver tone has fan-shaped black glass stones accented with light siam ab rhinestones; necklace is 16½" x 1⅛" and bracelet is 7⅛" x 1½", **$160.00 – 175.00.**
Mary Ann Docktor-Smith collection

Outstanding Boucher fur clip with matching earrings, likely from the late 1950s with open backed green cabochons and clear and blue rhinestones, each piece is signed. Clip is 2¾" x 1⅞" and clip earrings are 1⅞" x 1", **$295.00 – 350.00.** Jayne Spencer collection

Close-up of signature on back of fur clip.

Reverse view of set.

Here's a Claudette set you haven't seen before, at least in my books, it is a fabulous set with orange, clear aurora borealis, and smoky topaz stones, in a gun-metal setting, **$225.00 – 250.00.** Jayne Spencer collection

Spectacular unsigned saphiret set of bracelet with matching earrings, saphiret stones change color as you rotate them in different light, they are incredibly difficult to photograph and show the variety of color, this set is japanned black and has clip earrings, **$275.00 – 295.00.** Cheryl Killmer collection

Vendôme blue flower brooch with huge 1" blue AB rhinestone and matching earrings, brooch 3½" x 2¼", earrings 1¼" x 1", **$150.00 – 185.00.** Cheryl Killmer collection

Parures & Demi Parures

Close-up
view of mark.

Ravanna silver-plated imitation
pearl parure, necklace 17", pendant
4" x 2", brooch 3½" x 2", bracelet
2¼" diameter, earrings 1½" x ⅞",
$295.00 – 325.00. Cheryl Killmer
collection

HAR imitation pearl and teal aurora borealis
navettes, white finish, bracelet and earrings set,
$350.00 – 425.00. Cheryl Killmer collection

Reverse view showing signature.

Fenichel emerald and aurora borealis parure with necklace, bracelet, and earrings. All pieces have large prong-set rhinestones in emerald green, peacock blue aurora borealis, and clear with pink toned aurora borealis. Necklace is 15¾", bracelet is 7⅛", and earrings are 1" x ⅞", **$250.00 – 275.00.**
Dinah Taylor collection

Sterling triplet from the 1920s in amber color with flashes of blue, ring is size 6, bracelet is 7", and brooch is 1½", **$160.00 – 185.00.** Judy Miller collection

Rosaline and dark red pin and earrings set, brooch is 3" across, **$75.00 – 90.00.**
Judy Miller collection

Side view of earrings showing depth.

Miriam Haskell necklace and earrings set in lapis colored glass beads, necklace 17" and clip earrings are 1", **$450.00 – 495.00.** Judy Miller collection

Hobé cuff bracelet with clip earrings, bracelet is hinged, clips are 1¼", **$220.00 – 250.00.** Judy Miller collection

Judith McCann doubled triple strand necklace with green beads and blue and gold accents, necklace is adjustable to 23", frog clasp is marked "JUDITH MC-CANN," matching wingback earrings are 1¼" x 1", and there is a specified right earring and a specified left earring, **$175.00 – 195.00.** Sherry James collection

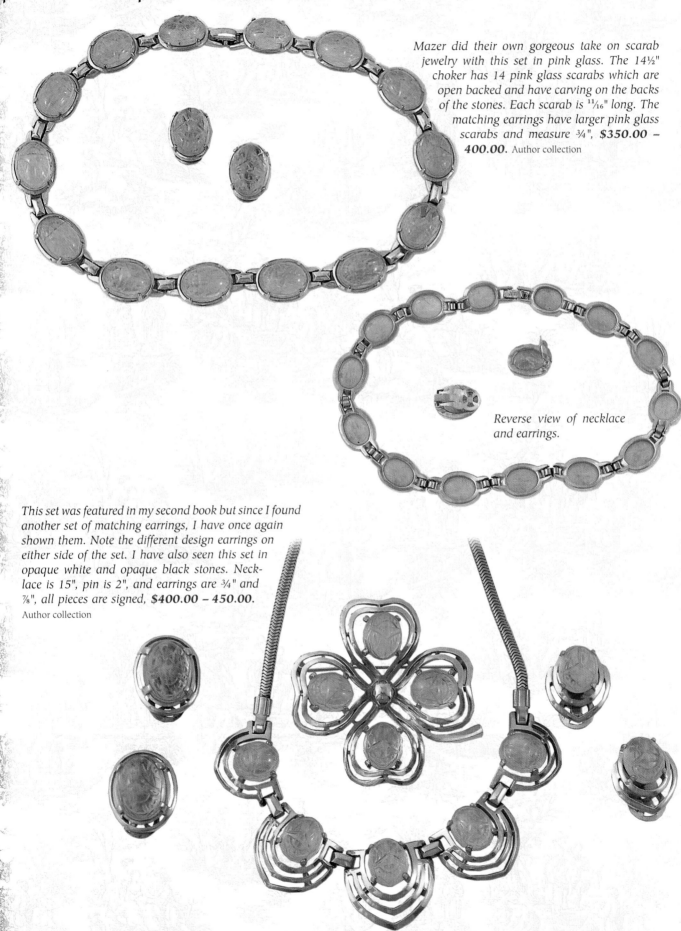

Mazer did their own gorgeous take on scarab jewelry with this set in pink glass. The 14½" choker has 14 pink glass scarabs which are open backed and have carving on the backs of the stones. Each scarab is ¹¹⁄₁₆" long. The matching earrings have larger pink glass scarabs and measure ¾", **$350.00 – 400.00.** Author collection

Reverse view of necklace and earrings.

This set was featured in my second book but since I found another set of matching earrings, I have once again shown them. Note the different design earrings on either side of the set. I have also seen this set in opaque white and opaque black stones. Necklace is 15", pin is 2", and earrings are ¾" and ⅞", all pieces are signed, **$400.00 – 450.00.**
Author collection

Napier white and gold bead bracelet and earrings set, with screw-on clip earrings, all pieces are signed, bracelet 8", earrings 2¼", **$40.00 – 55.00**. Author collection

This set looks just like Florenza with white glass, but it is unsigned, note earrings each have one person from the couple on them, pin is 2¼" tall and 1⅝" wide with a bale attached to wear as a pendant, earrings are 1¼" tall, **$25.00 – 45.00**. Author collection

Napier white beaded bracelet and earrings set, with screw-on clip earrings, bracelet is 7¾" and earrings have 10 mm beads, **$40.00 – 55.00**. Author collection

Here is a fun set of cowboy and cowgirl clothes with just the right accessories, boots and guns! This set was made by Donald Richard's for don-lin and I found the cowgirl outfit 10 years after I found the cowboy outfit. Each piece is articulated and sways and jingles when you wear them. Cowboy and cowgirl are both 5½" tall, cowgirl is signed "don-lin" but cowboy is not, however, since I purchased him and store him with his original card, I know he is a don-lin design too, **$100.00 – 125.00** for the pair, **$45.00 – 55.00** each. Author collection

Les Bernard matched set of lapis colored glass beads with black eyed panther clasps, each panther head has three glass cabochons in their collars and their eyes are black glass cabochons. Necklace is 34" long and can wrap around twice, bracelet is 8" long, the ring closes inside the panther's mouth and the clasp remains hidden under the panther head, only necklace is marked. This series came in a variety of animal heads and colored beads, **$150.00 – 165.00** for the set. Author collection

Photographs do not capture the warmth and beauty of this set by Les Bernard, the pearls have the warm glow of genuine pearls. The necklace is 16¼" with a hang tag attached and there are two pairs of identical earrings, one for pierced ears and the other has screw-on clip backs, the pierced earrings are not marked but the screw-on clips are both signed, earrings are 2¼" long, **$125.00 – 150.00** for the set. Author collection

Snowflake design matching pin with earrings from B. David, in business from 1945 to 1993, pin and one earring are signed, pin is 1½" in diameter, and earrings are 1" in diameter, **$55.00 – 75.00** for the set. Author collection

Reverse view showing signature.

Park Lane purple grapes cluster pin with matching clip earrings, only earrings are signed, all stones are prong set, pin is 1⅞" x 2", earrings are 1¼" tall, **$50.00 – 70.00.** Author collection

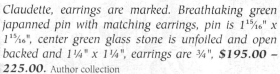

Claudette, earrings are marked. Breathtaking green japanned pin with matching earrings, pin is 1¹⁵⁄₁₆" x 1¹⁵⁄₁₆", center green glass stone is unfoiled and open backed and 1¼" x 1¼", earrings are ¾", **$195.00 – 225.00.** Author collection

Reverse view of pin.

Matching earrings to Hobé bracelet, earrings are clip and dangle nearly 3". Author collection

White plastic expansion bracelet with glass fruit beads and three rows of white plastic beads, centerpiece is 2" tall, though unsigned this is a Hobé design, I have seen the set with signed earrings, **$300.00 – 400.00** for the set. Author collection

This is an impressive well made set signed "Germany," the 7¼" bracelet has two gold tone, rhinestone, and pearl drops hanging from it, they hang to nearly 3". Earrings are clip with the same drop and they are 2" tall, a very elegant set, **$125.00 – 165.00**. Author collection

Bold and colorful set of bracelet with matching pin by Les Bernard, Inc., both pieces are signed. Bracelet has black glass stones and colored Lucite stones, the purple emerald cut stones have silver foiled backing, while the black stones are opaque and carved. Bracelet is 8" x ¾" and the pin is 4¼" tall, **$115.00 – 145.00**. Author collection

This unusual set has rhinestones, hand-wired beads, and enameling in a lovely floral spray design, and though clearly a set, only the earrings are marked "Robert." The pin is 2½" x 1¾" and the earrings are 1½" x 1", **$155.00 – 175.00.** Annie Navetta collection

This standout set of bracelet with matching earrings has a flower design accented with red marquise and ruby red cabochons, with pink aurora borealis chatons, bracelet is 7" x ⅞" and clip earrings are 1¼" in diameter. There are no marks but the clasp appears to have been replaced, where it was likely marked. Still a gorgeous and desirable set, **$125.00 – 155.00.** Annie Navetta collection

Pearly white thermoplastic demi parure with clear aurora borealis chaton accents, unsigned, 22" long, **$85.00 – 125.00** for the set. Annie Navetta collection

Matching bracelet, also unsigned, 6¾" x 1¼". Annie Navetta collection

Reverse view of pin set.

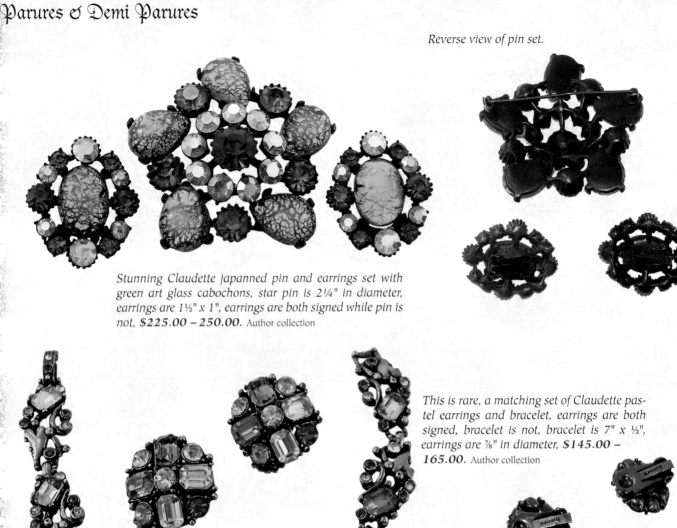

Stunning Claudette japanned pin and earrings set with green art glass cabochons, star pin is 2¼" in diameter, earrings are 1½" x 1", earrings are both signed while pin is not, **$225.00 – 250.00.** Author collection

This is rare, a matching set of Claudette pastel earrings and bracelet, earrings are both signed, bracelet is not, bracelet is 7" x ½", earrings are ⅞" in diameter, **$145.00 – 165.00.** Author collection

Great colorful Napier set of bracelet with clip and screw earrings, beads look like crackle glass, and have bumpy gold-tone beads, bracelet is 7" long and earrings are 1" in diameter, all pieces are signed, **$165.00 – 175.00.** Author collection

Brilliant red Claudette pin and earrings set, in gun metal, with pink aurora borealis chatons, earrings are both signed, pin is not, pin is 2⅛" x 2" and earrings are 1¼" x 1⅛", **$195.00 – 225.00.** Author collection

During the late 1980s a company named Art Deco produced a line of jewelry that copied vintage Cartier jewelry and sold in very high end department stores. This necklace and earrings set was made by them in 1989, as the attached tag is dated. The brown vase holding the flowers is Lucite, the vase is enameled and has red and clear rhinestone flowers. The necklace is 20" long with a centerpiece that is 4" x 3½", earrings are clips and are 1½" x 1¼" and are signed. The back of the necklace is also signed "Art Deco" twice. This set originally sold for **$800.00.** The Art Deco Company went out of business in the early 1990s, **$400.00 – 450.00.** Davida Baron collection/Photo courtesy of Davida Baron

Reverse view showing signature.

This set is unsigned but the workmanship and design say it is most likely French, it has gorgeous green iridescent art glass stones, and is possibly a 1950s design. Necklace is 13½" with a 2½" extender, the clip earrings dangle 2⅛" and the largest green stone is 1" long, **$300.00 – 350.00.** Davida Baron collection/ Photo courtesy of Davida Baron

Leo Glass magnificent festoon necklace with matching earrings, the flowery design is accented with pale blue glass stones, and has a pewter metal look. Chains drape along sides of necklace, necklace is 16" long, with a centerpiece 2½" x 2", screw earrings are ¾" x ½", **$250.00 – 295.00.** Davida Baron collection/Photo courtesy of Davida Baron

This festoon necklace and bracelet set, though unsigned, has been identified as a Joseff design, with five chains on the necklace anchoring a floral centerpiece with a large green glass stone, and seven chains on the bracelet with the same centerpiece. Necklace is 17½" with a centerpiece of 1½", and the bracelet is 6½" with a centerpiece of 1½", **$250.00 – 275.00.** Davida Baron collection/Photo courtesy of Davida Baron

Reverse view of the pair.

Antique bronze look necklace and earrings by Sandor, with purple and clear rhinestones, chains dangle Victorian style, signed "Sandor" on back of necklace centerpiece. Necklace is 15" long with a centerpiece that is 4" x 1¼", the clip earrings are 1½" x 1", **$175.00 – 195.00.** Davida Baron collection/Photo courtesy of Davida Baron

Parures & Demi Parures

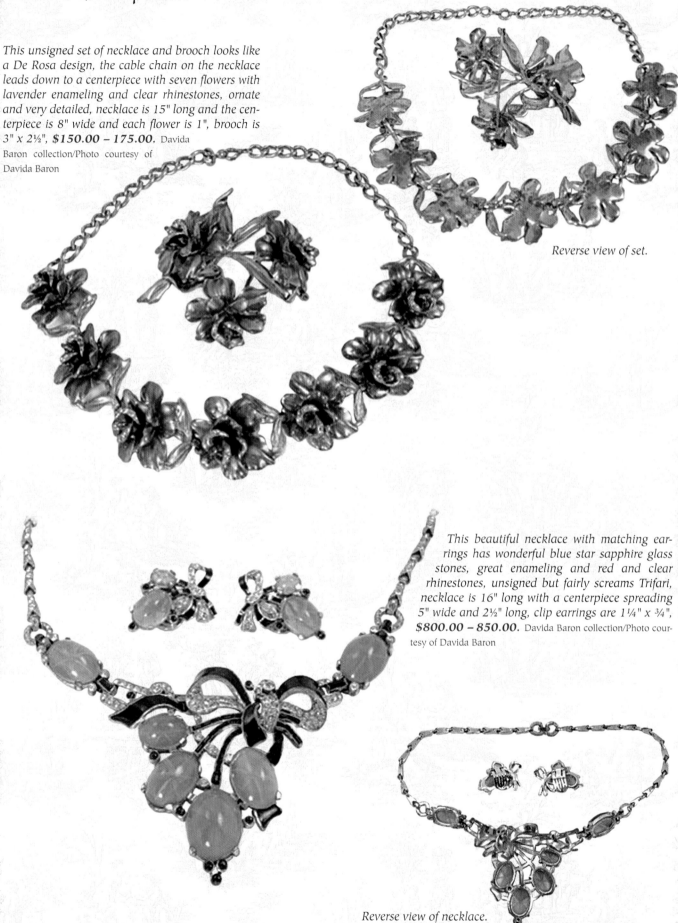

This unsigned set of necklace and brooch looks like a De Rosa design, the cable chain on the necklace leads down to a centerpiece with seven flowers with lavender enameling and clear rhinestones, ornate and very detailed, necklace is 15" long and the centerpiece is 8" wide and each flower is 1", brooch is 3" x 2½", **$150.00 – 175.00.** Davida Baron collection/Photo courtesy of Davida Baron

Reverse view of set.

This beautiful necklace with matching earrings has wonderful blue star sapphire glass stones, great enameling and red and clear rhinestones, unsigned but fairly screams Trifari, necklace is 16" long with a centerpiece spreading 5" wide and 2½" long, clip earrings are 1¼" x ¾", **$800.00 – 850.00.** Davida Baron collection/Photo courtesy of Davida Baron

Reverse view of necklace.

This is not a matched set but a marriage of dogwood blossom pin with dogwood blossom earrings, all unsigned, my daddy found the pin and a few months later found the earrings, dogwoods are gorgeous in spring time back in South Carolina. Pin is 3¾" x 1¾", and earrings are 1¼" in diameter, $35.00 – 45.00. Author collection

Hobé set of necklace with matching ear wraps, with mustard colored plastic pendant drop. Pendant is on a 22" gold-filled chain, ear wraps have 3" dangles with milk glass beads and crystal rhondelles, the original price tag is on the necklace and it says "Costumery Jewels by Hobé" and is priced at $10.00. All pieces signed, set, $195.00 – 265.00. Kim Paff collection/ Photo courtesy of www.kimsvintage.com

Beautiful Hobé autumn colors set, with 20" long necklace with beaded drop design, plus an extender of 3", centerpiece is also 3" long, clip earrings are 1¼" in diameter, all pieces signed, $150.00 – 175.00. Kim Paff collection/ Photo courtesy of www.kimsvintage.com

Fabulous rarely seen set by Hobé with the cuff bracelet, necklace, and clip earrings, all signed, 2¼" pendant is on a 22" chain, cuff is 2" wide and dangle earrings are 2" long, $350.00 – 450.00. Kim Paff collection/Photo courtesy of www.kimsvintage.com

Kunio Matsumoto for Trifari gold-tone set of necklace and clamper bracelet with root beer colored Lucite disks, pendant is 1⅝" on a 24" chain and disk on bracelet is 1⅝", all pieces signed, $175.00 – 200.00. Kim Paff collection/ Photo courtesy of www.kimsvintage.com

Kunio Matsumoto signatures on root beer set.

103

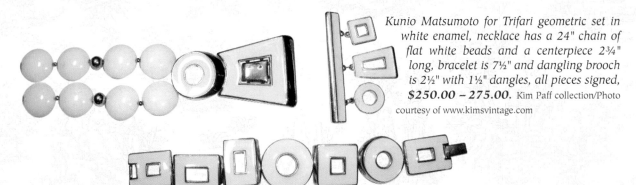

Kunio Matsumoto for Trifari geometric set in white enamel, necklace has a 24" chain of flat white beads and a centerpiece 2¾" long, bracelet is 7½" and dangling brooch is 2½" with 1½" dangles, all pieces signed, **$250.00 – 275.00.** Kim Paff collection/Photo courtesy of www.kimsvintage.com

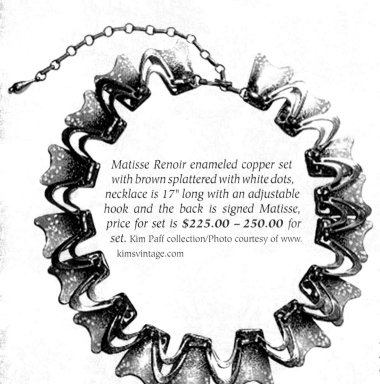

Kunio Matsumoto for Trifari turquoise colored Lucite set of necklace with matching earrings, necklace is 18" long with a 2" centerpiece, dangling pierced earrings on their original card are 2" long, all are signed, **$195.00 – 225.00.** Kim Paff collection/Photo courtesy of www.kimsvintage.com

Kunio Matsumoto for Trifari cuff bracelet with matching brooch with laminated Lucite centerpieces, which are clear on the top and painted white on the bottom, Lucite piece on bracelet is 1¾" x 1", brooch with its original hang tag is 1" x 2", both are signed, **$250.00 – 275.00.** Kim Paff collection/Photo courtesy of www.kimsvintage.com

Matisse Renoir enameled copper set with brown splattered with white dots, necklace is 17" long with an adjustable hook and the back is signed Matisse, price for set is **$225.00 – 250.00** for set. Kim Paff collection/Photo courtesy of www.kimsvintage.com

Matching earrings to previous necklace, screw back earrings are 1½" tall. Kim Paff collection/Photo courtesy of www.kimsvintage.com

Matisse Renoir set in forest green with necklace, pin, and earrings, all pieces signed, enameled copper, necklace is 13¼" with a 3½" extender, pin is 2⅛" x 1⅞", and clip earrings are 1¼" x ¾", $275.00 – 295.00. Kim Paff collection/Photo courtesy of www.kimsvintage.com

Matisse Renoir curvy enameled copper in dark blue with white splatters, necklace is 18" long with an adjustable hook, signed, earrings are ⅞" x ⅞" and are signed, $195.00 – 250.00. Kim Paff collection/Photo courtesy of www.kimsvintage.com

Matisse Renoir enameled copper cuff bracelet with matching earrings, with the enameled panel appearing to float inside the bracelet, signed, and 1½" at its widest, clip earrings are ¾" at the widest, $195.00 – 250.00. Kim Paff collection/Photo courtesy of www.kimsvintage.com

Matisse Renoir enameled copper necklace with matching earrings in forest green, commonly known as Cleopatra, necklace is 15" long, **$195.00 – 250.00.** Kim Paff collection/Photo courtesy of www.kimsvintage.com

Matisse Renoir copper necklace with red enamel geometric design, necklace is 14" with a 3" extender, clip earrings, **$195.00 – 250.00.** Kim Paff collection/Photo courtesy of www.kimsvintage.com

Signature tag for Matisse.

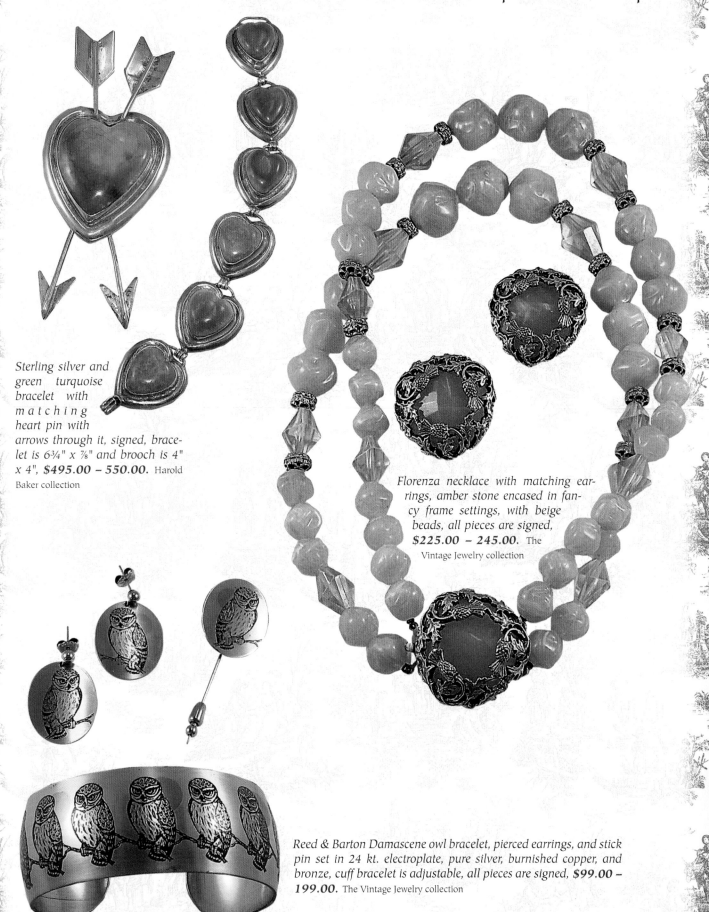

Sterling silver and green turquoise bracelet with m a t c h i n g heart pin with arrows through it, signed, brace-let is 6¾" x ⅞" and brooch is 4" x 4", **$495.00 – 550.00.** Harold Baker collection

Florenza necklace with matching ear-rings, amber stone encased in fan-cy frame settings, with beige beads, all pieces are signed, **$225.00 – 245.00.** The Vintage Jewelry collection

Reed & Barton Damascene owl bracelet, pierced earrings, and stick pin set in 24 kt. electroplate, pure silver, burnished copper, and bronze, cuff bracelet is adjustable, all pieces are signed, **$99.00 – 199.00.** The Vintage Jewelry collection

Necklaces

Reverse view of necklace.

Amethyst crystal choker necklace from the 1940s, heavy and solid, each link holds two amethyst baguette glass stones, and is 1" long, necklace is unsigned and 15½", **$150.00 – 175.00.**
Davida Baron collection/Photo courtesy of Davida Baron

Handmade emerald green necklace designed by Texan BeeGee McBride, a special design made exclusively for the owner. Necklace is made in three segments with gold-tone leaves, small green and citrine rhinestones, and large emerald shaped emerald green glass stones. Neck chain is made with green glass beads, necklace is 16" long with a centerpiece that is almost 3" long, signed with a metal hang tag saying "BG," **$225.00 – 250.00.** Davida Baron collection/Photo courtesy of Davida Baron

Retro necklace with five links holding oval faceted blue glass stones, surrounded by imitation pearls and pink rhinestones, necklace has an antique gold-tone metal finish, note chain with very ornate links leading up to hook clasp. Necklace is not signed but oddly has a hang tag attached meaning it was likely a designer piece, 14½" with a 2½" extender, **$100.00 – 125.00.** Davida Baron collection/ Photo courtesy of Davida Baron

Reverse view showing foiled and open backed stones.

This is a great example of early Czech workmanship, the design originated in the old Czech country where the combination of color crystals was designed for necklaces like this one. It is a festoon style with four rows of chains between glass crystals in pastel shades, all crystals are bezel set. Unsigned necklace is 16½" and the center falls 2½", slide-in clasp has same crystal design, **$300.00 – 350.00.** Davida Baron collection/Photo courtesy of Davida Baron

This is another early Czech necklace from the 1930s, in an antiqued gold finish with glass crystals set throughout, necklace has two chains leading to colorful stone slide-in clasp. Unsigned necklace is 19" long with a pendant center 2¾" x 1¾", **$125.00 – 150.00.** Davida Baron collection/Photo courtesy of Davida Baron

Copper necklace with blue moonstones has a great centerpiece with dangling chains, unsigned, necklace is 16" long and the centerpiece is 3" x 5¼", **$225.00 – 275.00.** Davida Baron collection/Photo courtesy of Davida Baron

T r e m e n - dous un-signed cross pendant with ruby red navettes and over-size cabochons, possibly an unsigned Hattie Carn-egie necklace, **$150.00 – 225.00.** Cheryl Killmer collection

Alice Caviness milk glass pendant necklace with huge gold-tone pendant of marquis, cabochon, and chaton stone in a variety of sizes, including one large 1" faceted stone, all stones are prong set and the largest three are open backed. The center flower has etched petals and a white chaton center while a wire work leaf adorns the top of the pendant. The 25" chain has a fold-over clasp, while the pendant is 2¾" in diameter and signed "Alice Caviness" on a cartouche, **$200.00 – 250.00.** Mary Ann Docktor-Smith collection

Reverse view of pendant.

Reverse view of cross.

Spectacular necklace with large emerald green glass set between rhinestone links, it is unsigned but could be either a Mazer or Trifari design, 14½", **$250.00 – 295.00.** Cheryl Killmer collection

Imitation pearl necklace with Art Deco convertible clasp/ brooch, necklace 14" long, clasp/brooch 2⅜" x 1¾", **$150.00 – 195.00.** Cheryl Killmer collection

1980s gold-tone and emerald green flat back and clear rhinestone heavy collar necklace, 15½" long x 1⅛" wide, **$200.00 – 250.00.** Cheryl Killmer collection

Reverse view of clasp/brooch.

Marvella 10 strand necklace of imitation pearls, jade, and sapphire beads with large yellow dentelle rhinestones, **$135.00 – 175.00.** Cheryl Killmer collection

Unsigned antiqued gold-tone drop necklace with pink and lavender rhinestones with one large unfoiled imitation amethyst stone in the center, possibly Robert or Hobé. Herringbone chain, 19", pendant 3¼" x 1½", **$150.00 – 195.00.** Cheryl Killmer collection

West German silver-tone necklace with large asymmetrical clear navettes, chatons, and imitation pearls with one large unfoiled faceted clear center stone. Necklace 17" long, pendant 2⅛" x 1⅝", **$250.00 – 300.00.** Cheryl Killmer collection

Deco style black beaded bow necklace, with a stunning 5¼" clear rhinestone bow centerpiece which is 2¼" wide, making the necklace a total of 18¼" long, **$175.00 – 225.00.** Cheryl Killmer collection

Vendôme black faceted beaded tassel necklace and earrings, necklace 27", tassel 4", earrings 1", **$135.00 – 165.00.** Cheryl Killmer collection

Rare Ben Meltzer Inc. N.Y. brass necklace and pendant with huge faceted green glass and cabochon pendant, chain 18", pendant 3½" x 3", **$175.00 – 195.00.** Cheryl Killmer collection

Rare Bellini rhodium-plated choker with clear rhinestones, similar in construction to Eisenberg, 16" long, **$225.00 – 250.00.** Cheryl Killmer collection

Napier Nouveau style silver-plated with purple cabochons parure, necklace 16" long x 1½" wide, bracelet 7" x 1¼", earrings, 1¾" x 1⅛", **$275.00 – 300.00.** Cheryl Killmer collection

Victorian carved amber pendant necklace with a dragon hunting a bird, seed pearls and 14 kt. findings, 19" long, **$160.00 – 185.00.** Judy Miller collection

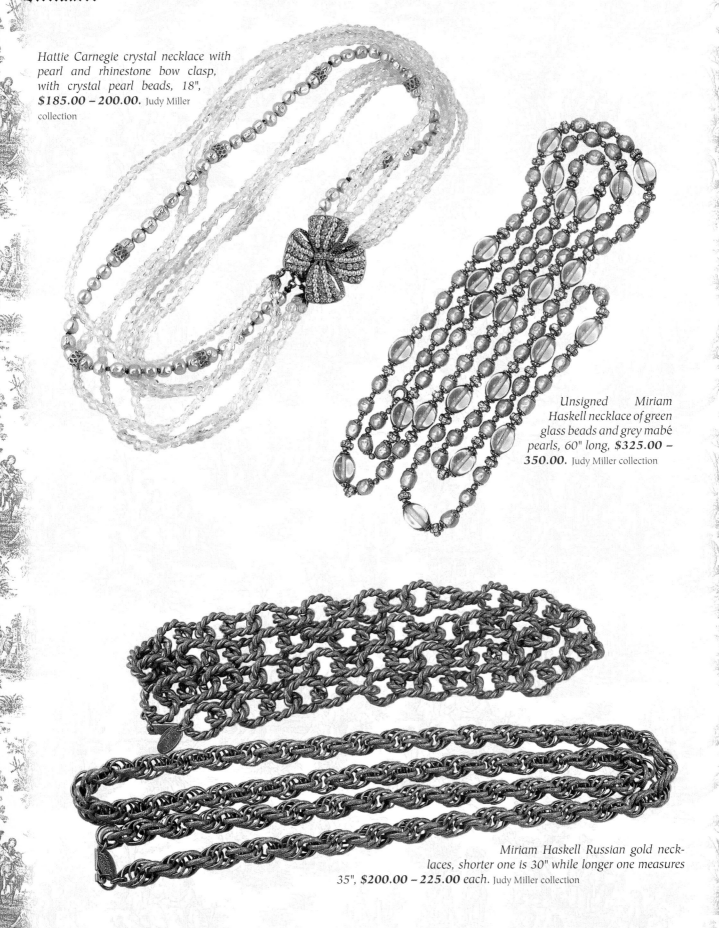

Hattie Carnegie crystal necklace with pearl and rhinestone bow clasp, with crystal pearl beads, 18", **$185.00 – 200.00.** Judy Miller collection

Unsigned Miriam Haskell necklace of green glass beads and grey mabé pearls, 60" long, **$325.00 – 350.00.** Judy Miller collection

Miriam Haskell Russian gold neck-laces, shorter one is 30" while longer one measures 35", **$200.00 – 225.00** each. Judy Miller collection

Miriam Haskell necklace by Larry Vrba in gold and pink, 31" long, $400.00 – 450.00. Judy Miller collection

Art Deco filigree necklace with paperclip chain and square blue glass stones, 19¼" long with filigree centerpiece 1½" x 1", $155.00 – 195.00. Author collection

A classic Mazer design with excellent quality rhinestones and imitation pearls, 15" long, and signed "Mazer Bros." on back of rhinestone clasp, $95.00 – 155.00. Author collection

Pink and green rhinestone necklace with round and marquise stones, unsigned, 15" long with a 1½" centerpiece, the bottom of which is attached to dangle and move, $85.00 – 95.00. Author collection

Coro pink moonstone necklace on box chain with leaves accented with clear rhinestones, signed "Coro" and "Pat. Pend." on back, 14¾" long, drop is 1¼", $65.00 – 85.00. Author collection

Les Bernard heavy glass beaded necklace with imitation pearls, rhondelles, and red melon glass beads, 28", signed "Les Bernard Inc." with hang tag, $65.00 – 85.00. Author collection

115

Sassy black and white ceramic cat necklace by Candace Loheed for Ruby Z, cat centerpiece is 4" tall and 2" wide, signed on bead close to barrel clasp, necklace is 21" long, **$125.00 – 150.00**. Author collection

Ceramic jungle cat in black and white by Candace Loheed for Ruby Z, jungle cat is 2½" x 1¾", signed on bead near clasp, necklace is 18" long, **$125.00 – 150.00**. Author collection

Colorful beaded ceramic Holstein cow necklace by Candace Loheed for Ruby Z, cow is 3" x 2", necklace is 24", **$125.00 – 150.00** if perfect. Author collection

Fabulous ceramic bananas necklace with black and yellow beads, note beads next to bananas have white dots, each banana is 2" long and the centerpiece of bananas stretches nearly 5", necklace is 17" long and signed "Flying Colors," **$175.00 – 225.00**. Author collection

This ceramic necklace has beads that appear to have a jungle striped theme to them, in red with black and white, by Candace Loheed for Ruby Z, this is a much longer necklace than is usually found in the California ceramic jewelry lines, necklace is 34" long and the red and black beads are each 2" long, **$125.00 – 150.00.** Author collection

Piggy nursery rhyme ceramic necklace by Flying Colors, piggy on left is heading towards the market while piggy on right is heading home at a fast clip, necklace is signed on back of center piggy with bib, fork, and knife and also on the heart-shaped bead next to the clasp. Piggies are 1½" to 2" and necklace is 18", **$175.00 – 225.00.** Author collection

Colorful ceramic beaded necklace with little white ducks, by Parrot Pearls, little ducks are 1" wide, necklace is 16" long and signed on round bead near clasp, Parrot Pearls jewelry is harder to find than Ruby Z or Flying Colors, **$150.00 – 175.00.** Author collection

Flying Colors holly and berries ceramic Christmas necklace with metal silvertone beads, signed on back of holly leaves, centerpiece is 3" x 2", necklace is 18", **$75.00 – 95.00.** Author collection

Startled little ceramic pig necklace by Flying Colors with pink dotted beads, piggy is signed on back, and is 2" x 1½", necklace is 15", **$75.00 – 95.00.** Author collection

This Bohemian necklace features bezel-set dangling crystals which are 1½" long, a chain divided by small crystal beads, the centerpiece of Victorian design is 6½" wide, unsigned, note the tiny flower design, from the 1920s, **$250.00 – 275.00.** Davida Baron collection/Photo courtesy of Davida Baron

Bohemian necklace from the 1920s or 1930s with Victorian-style charms holding bezel-set glass stones, note filigree beads, necklace is 17" long and the longest charm is 2¼", **$250.00 – 275.00.**
Davida Baron collection/Photo courtesy of Davida Baron

Unusual Goldette bib necklace with amethyst faceted glass stones, in an antiqued gold finish, all stones are unfoiled, necklace is 14½" long and the longest crystal dangle is 4" long, **$125.00 – 145.00.** Davida Baron collection/Photo courtesy of Davida Baron

View showing signature mark.

Gorgeous enameled necklace with lovely pink rhinestones, possibly European and from the 1930s, unsigned, necklace is 17" long, centerpiece design is 6" x 2", **$225.00 – 250.00.** Davida Baron collection/Photo courtesy of Davida Baron

Regal and ornate Bohemian necklace with a huge centerpiece with glass stones and cabochons, likely from the 1930s, necklace is 15" long with a centerpiece 4¼" x 2½", **$400.00 – 450.00.** Davida Baron collection/Photo courtesy of Davida Baron

Bohemian necklace with purple glass stones in an antiqued gold finish, from the 1930s, necklace is 19" long with a centerpiece 3" x 1½", highly ornate design on centerpiece and chain, **$300.00 – 350.00.** Davida Baron collection/ Photo courtesy of Davida Baron

Sandor bib necklace with bezel-set green glass stones, signed "Sandor" on the hook, each link has a very intricate design surrounding the green stones, likely dates to the 1940s, necklace is 15" long with the centerpiece design being 6" x 3½", **$150.00 – 195.00.** Davida Baron collection/ Photo courtesy of Davida Baron

Reverse view of Sandor necklace.

Fabulous Trifari pink bib necklace with pink stone arrows, accented with clear rhinestones, signed "Trifari" and "Pat. Pend." on clasp, necklace is 15" long and the centerpiece is 3½" wide and the longest dangle is 3½" long, **$200.00 – 250.00.** Davida Baron collection/Photo courtesy of Davida Baron

Reverse view of Trifari necklace.

Czech choker with large faceted pink glass stones accented with tiny green stones inside a leaf pattern, great necklace from the 1930s, it is 14½" and the centerpiece is 2¾" in diameter, **$300.00 – 350.00.** Davida Baron collection/Photo courtesy of Davida Baron

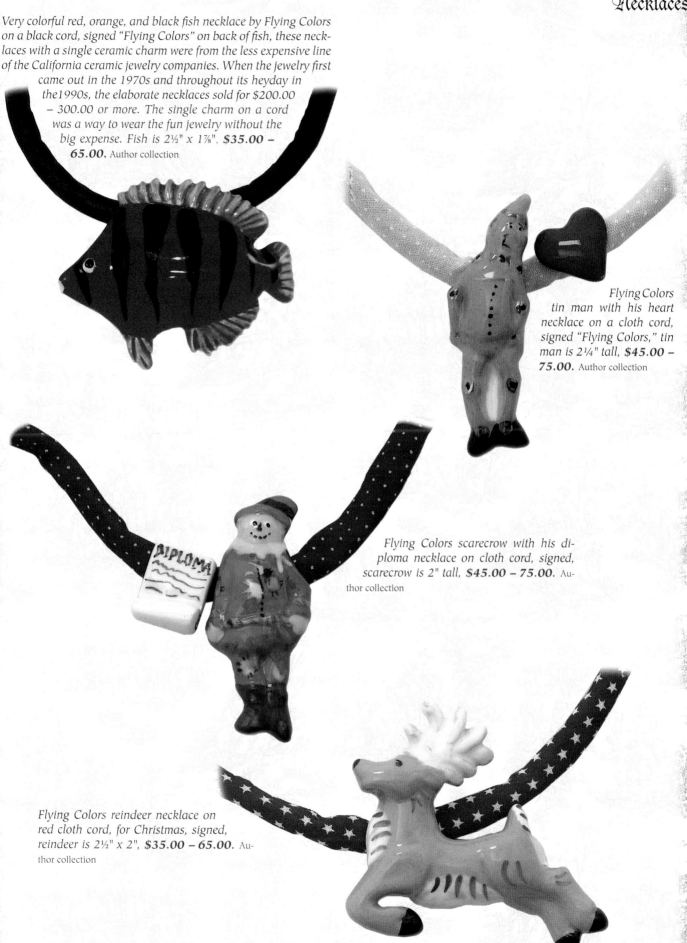

Very colorful red, orange, and black fish necklace by Flying Colors on a black cord, signed "Flying Colors" on back of fish, these necklaces with a single ceramic charm were from the less expensive line of the California ceramic jewelry companies. When the jewelry first came out in the 1970s and throughout its heyday in the1990s, the elaborate necklaces sold for $200.00 – 300.00 or more. The single charm on a cord was a way to wear the fun jewelry without the big expense. Fish is 2½" x 1⅞", **$35.00 – 65.00.** Author collection

Flying Colors tin man with his heart necklace on a cloth cord, signed "Flying Colors," tin man is 2¼" tall, **$45.00 – 75.00.** Author collection

Flying Colors scarecrow with his diploma necklace on cloth cord, signed, scarecrow is 2" tall, **$45.00 – 75.00.** Author collection

Flying Colors reindeer necklace on red cloth cord, for Christmas, signed, reindeer is 2½" x 2", **$35.00 – 65.00.** Author collection

121

Incredible two-strand charm necklace from Zoe Coste, signed "Zoe Coste Made in France," necklace has 18 charms with a Tex-Mex theme, and including Native American Indian charms. Shorter strand is 17" long, note the Eyes of Texas map charm, longest charm is 1¾", **$250.00 – 295.00.** Author collection

Ruby Z ceramic heart necklace made by Candace Loheed, signature bead has "Ruby Z" on one side and "Candace Loheed" on the other, crazed pattern is in the design, it is not an aging effect, 2⅞" x 3⅛", **$125.00 – 150.00.** Author collection

Kunio Matsumoto for Trifari silver-tone necklace with colored Lucite centerpiece design, largest blue piece is 2" long and 1" wide at its widest point, 16" long, signed, **$125.00 – 150.00.** Kim Paff collection/Photo courtesy of www.kimsvintage.com

Kunio Matsumoto for Trifari torsade necklace with clear and black beads, with rhinestone centerpiece, necklace is 18" long and centerpiece is 1½", signed, **$145.00 – 195.00.** Kim Paff collection/Photo courtesy of www.kimsvintage. com

Kunio Matsumoto for Trifari geometric necklace in black with rhinestone accents, necklace is 15" long and centerpiece is 1½", signed, **$125.00 – 150.00.** Kim Paff collection/Photo courtesy of www.kimsvintage.com

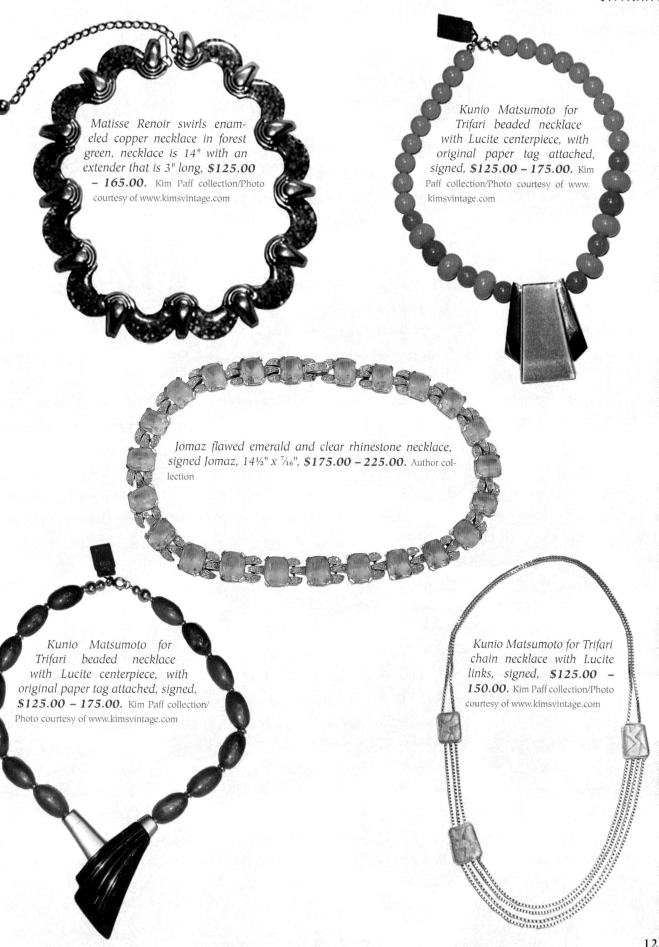

Matisse Renoir swirls enameled copper necklace in forest green, necklace is 14" with an extender that is 3" long, **$125.00 – 165.00.** Kim Paff collection/Photo courtesy of www.kimsvintage.com

Kunio Matsumoto for Trifari beaded necklace with Lucite centerpiece, with original paper tag attached, signed, **$125.00 – 175.00.** Kim Paff collection/Photo courtesy of www. kimsvintage.com

Jomaz flawed emerald and clear rhinestone necklace, signed Jomaz, 14½" x ⁷⁄₁₆", **$175.00 – 225.00.** Author collection

Kunio Matsumoto for Trifari beaded necklace with Lucite centerpiece, with original paper tag attached, signed, **$125.00 – 175.00.** Kim Paff collection/ Photo courtesy of www.kimsvintage.com

Kunio Matsumoto for Trifari chain necklace with Lucite links, signed, **$125.00 – 150.00.** Kim Paff collection/Photo courtesy of www.kimsvintage.com

Bracelets

Selro rhinestone and cabochon bracelet, features five linked and riveted design elements, including a butterfly, a large square cabochon, an Asian gentleman, a dragonfly, and a coiled snake. These intricate motifs are set with many different shapes of rhinestones, cabochons, and ballotini (undrilled pearls). Though this bracelet is not marked, it clearly matches other marked Selro pieces. Bracelet is 7¾" x 1¼", **$240.00 – 275.00.** Mary Ann Docktor-Smith collection

Reverse view of bracelet.

Hollycraft 1953 pastel bracelet in gold tone with an enchanting mix of stone colors and shapes, with a fold-over clasp and safety chain, 7" x ⅞", **$120.00 – 145.00.** Mary Ann Docktor-Smith collection

Reverse view of bracelet.

Impressive Tortolani gold-tone bracelet with a wheat sheaf motif and the high quality construction this company is known for; it measures 7⅜" x 1⅛", and is signed "Tortolani" in script on a tear-drop cartouche, **$75.00 – 95.00.** Mary Ann Docktor-Smith collection

Reverse view of bracelet.

This elegant bracelet could be an unsigned Selro or Selini, it definitely has the look, with its Lucite cabochons filled with confetti, bracelet is 7¼" x 1⅝", $115.00 – 135.00. Cheryl Killmer collection

This remarkable bracelet has large flawed emerald cabochons and is surrounded by round and marquise rhinestones in pale green and canary yellow, unsigned, 7", $195.00 – 250.00. Cheryl Killmer collection

Renaissance style bracelet of heavy gun metal with light gray imitation pearls and blue-gray ovals and chatons, 7" x 1⅝", $115.00 – 135.00. Cheryl Killmer collection

Jomaz flawed emerald and clear rhinestone bracelet, 7" x½", $150.00 – 175.00. Author collection

Jomaz gold-plated chunky bracelet with huge dark green Lucite cabochons 1⅛" long, bracelet is 7½" and is marked "JOMAZ" with the copyright symbol, $110.00 – 135.00. Cheryl Killmer collection

*Hobé nine row rhinestones, black with emerald green baguettes, 1950s, 7⅜" x 1⅜", **$110.00 – 125.00.*** Cheryl Killmer collection

*Unsigned gold-plated bracelet, possibly Trifari, with invisibly set ruby and clear rhinestones, 7⅜" x ⅝", **$150.00 – 195.00.*** Cheryl Killmer collection

*Art Deco pot-metal bracelet with dark blue cushion-cut square stones and clear rhinestones, 7½" x ¹⁵⁄₁₆", **$125.00 – 150.00.*** Cheryl Killmer collection

I never could get a good photograph of this stunning amethyst bracelet, I guess you just have to see it to appreciate it. The amethyst emerald-cut stones have unfoiled backs and are prong set and open backed, with aurora borealis accent stones on each link. Each link holds four large stones, and each end has dark blue marquis stones and round ab stones, even the clasp has a prong set blue marquise stone. Bracelet is 6½" with a 2¼" extension and a safety chain. The back is as well designed as the front, **$95.00 – 125.00.** Author collection

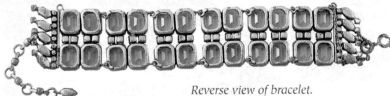

Reverse view of bracelet.

Napier bracelets remain strongly sought after by collectors, and here is one of the single charm designs, with an elephant in full regalia, with imitation pearl dangles and glass beads, bracelet is 7¾" long, and elephant charm is 1½" tall, bracelet is marked on back of clasp and under elephant, $50.00 – 75.00. Author collection

I call this Napier bracelet my "Mentos" bracelet because the white plastic disks look like the candy mints. The bracelet is 7⅓" long and the disks are ¾" each. Fold-over clasp is signed, $75.00 – 85.00. Author collection

This great bracelet is a souvenir charm bracelet from San Francisco and includes charms of Coit Tower, the bridge, and a cable car. Bracelet is 7½" long and the longest charm is Coit Tower at 1¼", $40.00 – 55.00. Author collection

I started this charm bracelet 20 years ago when I went to Disney-World. Most of the charms are sterling, there are also two gold-tone charms with rhinestones. Note Cinderella's pumpkin coach in the middle. Bracelet is 8" long and the pumpkin coach is ⅞" long, $100.00 – 125.00. Author collection

Florida souvenir enameled charm bracelet with a dolphin, palm tree, alligator, flamingo, sailfish, and surfer, 6½" long, $20.00 – 30.00. Author collection

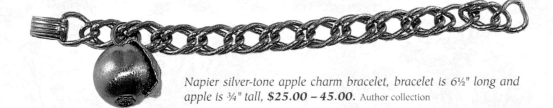

Napier silver-tone apple charm bracelet, bracelet is 6½" long and apple is ¾" tall, **$25.00 – 45.00.** Author collection

The first place I went to visit when I moved to Las Vegas was M&M World, because I secretly collect M&M candy dispensers and figurals. I wanted a charm bracelet loaded with charms but the only ones they had were for kids and had only four charms on them. I bought two and made the perfect size for my wrist but still need-ed extra charms. The one with rhinestones was $30.00 and it only came with one charm. I went over to the key chains and found some that had six tiny charms on them for $5 each, so I bought a couple and added all of those charms to the bracelet. Now it is filled with great looking M&M charms in all the colors and with different signs. Bracelet is 7½" long, but I think it needs a few more charms! This is how you have fun with a charm bracelet. **$60.00 – 75.00.** Author collection

Charm bracelet with large crown charms that have either cabochons or large round rhine-stones, two crowns have pearl accents, un-signed, bracelet is 7" long, **$65.00 – 85.00.** Author collection

Souvenir charm bracelet from Hawaii has enameled flower charms and a Hawaiian crest charm on a bracelet of imitation pearls, 7¼", **$25.00 – 45.00.** Author collection

Another Disney themed charm bracelet, this one with characters from The Little Mermaid, each charm except for Ariel's father is marked "Disney," bracelet is 7" long, **$25.00 – 45.00.** Author collection

This charm bracelet has eggs reminiscent of Fabergé eggs, and gold cage beads, bracelet is 7½" long and the red center charm is 1" tall, **$55.00 – 65.00.** Author collection

Back in the mid 1990s Monet came out with charms that had a spring ring attached and you could buy any charm to instantly add to a bracelet, this bracelet is 7½" long with five charms including a mustard seed charm, **$25.00 – 45.00.** Author collection

Carolee heraldic charm bracelet in gold-tone metal, 8" long with Carolee hang tag. Carolee has a worldwide lifetime guarantee on their jewelry and will make any repairs necessary. Note bracelet is adjustable with thinner rings near the end for the catch to fasten on, **$45.00 – 65.00.** Author collection

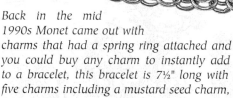

Cute little seashell themed Florida souvenir charm bracelet, 6½", **$10.00 – 25.00.** Author collection

Bracelets

Hollywood souvenir charm bracelet with some great charms including the Hollywood Bowl and the Farmers Market, 6½" long, **$20.00 – 35.00.** Author collection

Beautiful Carolee floral charm bracelet in gold tone, with 10 flower charms, half of the charms have imitation pearl or rhinestone accents, bracelet is 7" long with a toggle clasp, **$65.00 – 75.00.** Author collection

Sarah Coventry bracelet with cat's eye glass cabochons with bands of color, each is supposed to look different for a "real" look, 7½" long with a safety chain, **$15.00 – 20.00.** Author collection

Elegant purple glass grape cluster bracelet from Napier, grape cluster is nearly 2" tall, fold-over clasp is signed, **$75.00 – 95.00.** Author collection

Fabulous black and white design from Napier, all glass beads, with black and white art glass beads, clasp is signed, 7½", **$95.00 – 125.00.** Author collection

Very unusual design bracelet with prong-set green rhinestones, the two marquise stones are open backed, and there are two metal swirls accenting the top of the bracelet, with safety chain, 7" x ¾", **$75.00 – 95.00.** Author collection

Reverse view of bracelet.

Weiss clear rhinestone bracelet with all emerald-cut stones, three rows of stones, all prong set, 7¼" x ½", **$125.00 – 150.00.** Author collection

Reverse view of bracelet.

This one's a stunner, it is a Crown Trifari bracelet with red and clear rhinestones, extremely well made, 7" x ½", **$250.00 – 295.00.** Author collection

Reverse view of bracelet.

Oriental theme charm bracelet, each link is different, with green glass beads, unsigned but very well made, 7" x 1¾", **$95.00 – 125.00.** Author collection

131

Bracelets

Napier bracelet with bronze moonstone Lucite baubles, bracelet is signed and is 7½" long with 1½" bronze moonstone baubles, a classic Napier design, these baubles came in different colors such as blue, lavender, and pink, and gold tone and silver tone. **$95.00 – 125.00.** Author collection

Napier large black plastic bead charm style bracelet, 7½" x 1⅜", **$65.00 – 85.00.** Author collection

This beautifully designed bracelet features moonstone shoe button cabochons with rhinestone centers, this bracelet has unfortunately had its clasp replaced so it is unsigned, but similar to Trifari and Coro shoe button designed jewelry. Bracelet is 7" x 1" and shoe button cabochons are open backed, **$95.00 – 125.00.** Author collection

Close-up view of signature on bracelet.

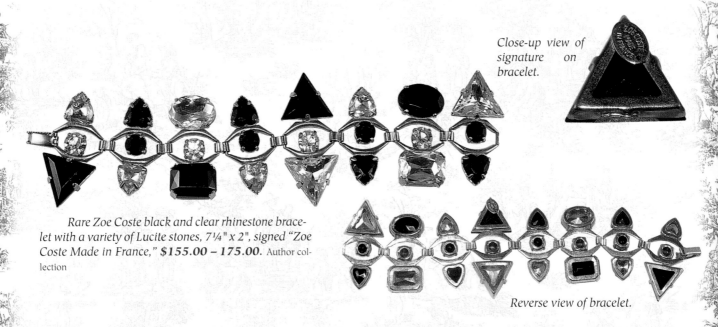

Rare Zoe Coste black and clear rhinestone bracelet with a variety of Lucite stones, 7¼" x 2", signed "Zoe Coste Made in France," **$155.00 – 175.00.** Author collection

Reverse view of bracelet.

Napier charm style bracelet with a cluster of Lucite and gold-tone beads on one end, bracelet is signed "Napier" on the underneath of the toggle, a fun design, 8" with a bead drop of 2", **$85.00 – 95.00.** Author collection

Les Bernard clear rhinestone hinged bangle bracelet, rhinestones go all the way around, these bracelets match the articulated flower pins, signed "Les Bernard Inc." on the inside hinge, bracelet is ½" wide, $95.00 – 125.00. Author collection

Green and blue rhinestone hinged bangle bracelet by Les Bernard, same as the bracelet at left, it matches the green and blue flower pin, and even has matching earrings. Bracelet is signed, $120.00 – 145.00. Author collection

This is a very oddly designed bracelet with clear and blue baguette rhinestones, the blue stones stand upright, bracelet has a safety chain and a push in clasp that has a blue stone on it, 7" x ⅜" and ½" high, unsigned, two blue baguettes sit in "center" of design, $150.00 – 175.00. Author collection

Side view showing depth and design of bracelet.

Incredible Art Deco bracelet with tall green glass cabochons, clear baguettes, and clear chatons, with push-in clasp, this 7" x 1¼" bracelet mimics the real thing. Green glass cabochons are open backed, bracelet is unsigned, safety chain is missing, $350.00 – 400.00. Author collection

Reverse view of bracelet.

Trifari gold-tone bracelet with oval and round rhinestones, 7" x ⁷⁄₁₆", $65.00 – 85.00. Author collection

Reverse view of bracelet.

133

Bracelets

Clear crackle glass buttons with green glass leaves make up this delicate 7½" bracelet, **$35.00 – 45.00.** Author collection

Tennis style bracelet with dark green square rhinestones and a belt buckle accent, slide-in clasp, unsigned, 7", **$55.00 – 75.00.** Author collection

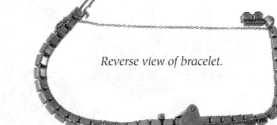

Reverse view of bracelet.

The clear rhinestones in this bracelet fairly glow, accented with pale blue oval stones in the centerpiece, unsigned, with push-in clasp, 7½" with 1" centerpiece, emerald-cut stones and blue stones are foiled and open backed, **$55.00 – 65.00.** Author collection

Clear rhinestone bracelet by Boucher, signed and numbered 6092, with safety chain, 7", **$95.00 – 125.00.** Author collection

Reverse view of bracelet.

Hattie Carnegie hinged cuff bracelet with imitation pearls and rhinestones, signed, 2½" tall, **$395.00 – 425.00.** The Vintage Jewelry collection

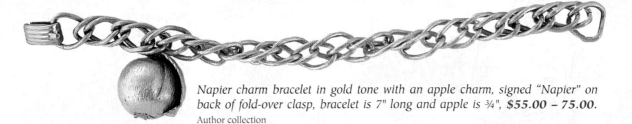

Napier charm bracelet in gold tone with an apple charm, signed "Napier" on back of fold-over clasp, bracelet is 7" long and apple is ¾", $55.00 – 75.00. Author collection

This is truly a rare find, a ceramic Parrot Pearls bracelet, signed "Parrot Pearls 1980," in a sheet music design. Candace Loheed of Parrot Pearls told me they rarely made bracelets because they were prone to damage from banging into things while wearing them. This bracelet has ceramic beads with the sheet music separated by squared off round beads, the sheet music beads are ½" wide, and bracelet is strung on elastic, in 10 years of collecting California ceramic jewelry, this is the first bracelet I have ever seen, $150.00 – 200.00. Author collection

Gold-tone chain bracelet with jade green cabochons and gold and white speckled larger cabochons, unsigned, 7" x ½", $55.00 – 75.00. Author collection

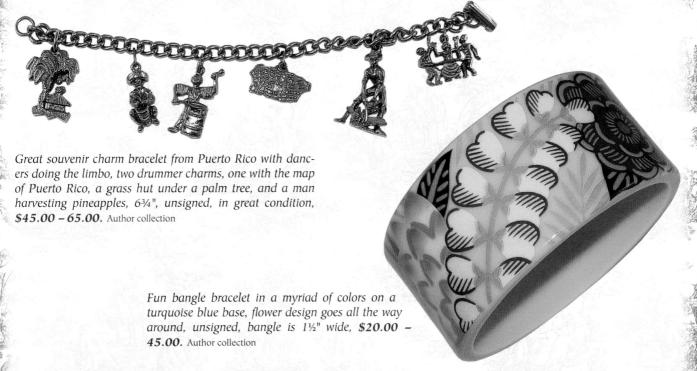

Great souvenir charm bracelet from Puerto Rico with dancers doing the limbo, two drummer charms, one with the map of Puerto Rico, a grass hut under a palm tree, and a man harvesting pineapples, 6¾", unsigned, in great condition, $45.00 – 65.00. Author collection

Fun bangle bracelet in a myriad of colors on a turquoise blue base, flower design goes all the way around, unsigned, bangle is 1½" wide, $20.00 – 45.00. Author collection

Bracelets

Beautiful leaf bracelet with carved glass stones, foiled and open backed, unsigned, 7" x ¾", $85.00 – 125.00. Author collection

Reverse view of bracelet.

Multicolored rhinestones link bracelet in antiqued gold-tone finish, with fold-over clasp, unsigned, 7½" x ¾", design looks like a slide bracelet but it is not, $65.00 – 85.00. Author collection

Matisse Renoir enameled copper cuff bracelet, signed, $95.00 – 125.00. Kim Paff collection/Photo courtesy of www.kimsvintage.com

Matisse Renoir copper bracelets with huge prong set cabochon stones, one in all white and the other multicolored, 1⅝" at its widest, $95.00 – 125.00 each. Kim Paff collection/Photo courtesy of www.kimsvintage.com

Kunio Matsumoto for Trifari hinged cuff bracelet with black enameled leaves and imitation pearls, $125.00 – 150.00. Kim Paff collection/ Photo courtesy of www.kimsvintage.com

Kunio Matsumoto for Trifari hinged cuff bracelet with blue and gray Lucite centerpieces, $125.00 – 150.00. Kim Paff collection/Photo courtesy of www.kimsvintage.com

Brooches & Pins

This is a Coro design rarely seen, a bird on a flowering branch, signed "Coro Craft Sterling" with a gold wash over the sterling, this is an Adolph Katz design, patent number 133,728 dated September 8, 1942. It is 2¼" x 2", **$295.00 – 350.00.** Author collection

Reverse view of brooch.

Made in France brass dress clip with raspberry glass, 1¾" across, attributed to Gripoix, **$225.00 – 250.00.** Judy Miller collection

Fabulous Bakelite anchor with life preserver pin, 2½", **$400.00 – 450.00.** Judy Miller collection

Eisenberg Ice orange wreath style brooch accented with clear rhinestones, 2⅜" x 1⅞", **$150.00 – 195.00.** Cheryl Killmer collection

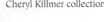

Reverse view showing signature.

HAR swan with ruby eyes and pavé rhine-stone body, signed "HAR," 2¾" x 1½", **$110.00 – 125.00.** Mary Ann Docktor-Smith collection

Reverse view of swan pin.

Lisner frosted oak leaves brooch in silver tone with Lucite leaves accented with ab rhinestones, 3" x 2" and marked "Lisner," **$40.00 – 55.00.** Mary Ann Docktor-Smith collection

Reverse view of brooch.

Appealing rhinestone floral spray pin is unmarked though it has elements of Coro floral designs, note the flowers inside the flowers that on Coro pins are tremblers, but here are riveted and stationary. A bit of the black enameling on the stems has worn away but pin is still quite lovely, 2½" x 1⅞", **$75.00 – 95.00.** Mary Ann Docktor-Smith collection

Reverse view of pin.

This sweet little pin has a secret, it is a very rare day to night convertible pin that can be worn as a simple circle pin or converted to a rhinestone-studded version by sliding the gold tone circle to the back of the pin, 1⅜" in diameter, **$75.00 – 95.00.** Mary Ann Docktor-Smith collection

Reverse view of pin.

Inviting Regency rhine-stone starfish pin with amethyst, olivine, fuchsia, and light sapphire stones surrounded by a rope effect, 2⅜" in diameter and marked "REGENCY" in an oval cartouche, **$50.00 – 75.00.** Mary Ann Docktor-Smith collection

Reverse view of pin.

Summery pot-metal rhinestone and enamel flower pin with deep red moonglow cabochons and ribbed handle, 2½" x 2½". Note non-enameled flower with green rhinestone center, **$95.00 – 125.00.** Mary Ann Docktor-Smith collection

Reverse view of pin.

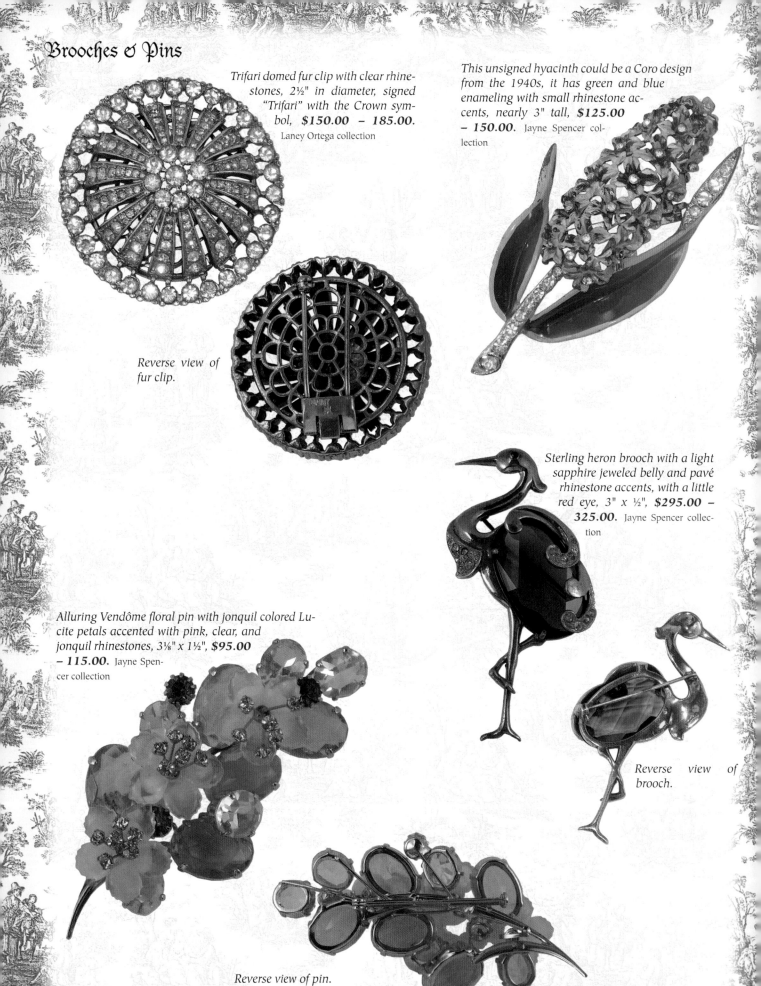

Brooches & Pins

Trifari domed fur clip with clear rhinestones, 2½" in diameter, signed "Trifari" with the Crown symbol, **$150.00 – 185.00.** Laney Ortega collection

This unsigned hyacinth could be a Coro design from the 1940s, it has green and blue enameling with small rhinestone accents, nearly 3" tall, **$125.00 – 150.00.** Jayne Spencer collection

Reverse view of fur clip.

Sterling heron brooch with a light sapphire jeweled belly and pavé rhinestone accents, with a little red eye, 3" x ½", **$295.00 – 325.00.** Jayne Spencer collection

Alluring Vendôme floral pin with jonquil colored Lucite petals accented with pink, clear, and jonquil rhinestones, 3⅛" x 1½", **$95.00 – 115.00.** Jayne Spencer collection

Reverse view of brooch.

Reverse view of pin.

Unsigned leaping swordfish brooch in pot metal with rhinestone accents and a blue eye, 3¼" x 3", **$225.00 – 250.00.** Jayne Spencer collection

Reverse view of pin.

Unsigned stylized japanned bow pin in green, likely from the 1960s, 3¼" x 3", **$145.00 – 165.00.** Jayne Spencer collection

Reverse view showing signature.

Kalinger (sometimes Kalinger Paris) gold-tone strawberry/fruit with yellow Lucite flowers and green beaded worm. 3½" x 1½", **$110.00 – 135.00.** Cheryl Killmer collection

Angry bird peering down at prey, this design looks like a Boucher but is unsigned, 4" tall, **$145.00 – 195.00.** Cheryl Killmer collection

Unsigned gold-plated flower pin with aquamarine and clear rhinestones, 5" x 2½", **$195.00 – 250.00.** Cheryl Killmer collection

141

Brooches & Pins

Sandor Sterling flower and vase pin with pink navette rhinestones, green baguettes, clears, and enameled leaves, 2¾" x 2¼", **$195.00 – 225.00.**
Cheryl Killmer collection

View showing signature.

Reverse view of pin.

Larry Vrba Christmas tree pin circa 1997, gun-metal frame with multicolored rhinestones and wired over star, 4¾" x 3", $175.00 – 225.00.
Cheryl Killmer collection

Larry Vrba Christmas tree pin circa 1997, gun-metal frame with different shades of green and purple stones, 4½" x 3", $175.00 – 225.00. Cheryl Killmer collection

Rhodium-plated Eisenberg flower spray with unfoiled red cushion-cut glass stones and clears, marked "Eisenberg Ice 2000" in script, 4½" x 2½", **$200.00 – 225.00.** Cheryl Killmer collection

Beautiful white enameled Hollycraft Christmas ornament brooch with ornaments hanging from a branch, 2½" x 1¾", **$45.00 – 75.00.** Jayne Spencer collection

Unique devil face brooch with sea creature design, wonderfully crafted, note tiny "nub" horns on devil's face, this brooch is made of two layers and is ⅝" deep, with stones that mimic genuine stones, brooch is 2⅛" in diameter, unsigned, **$150.00 – 175.00.** Cheryl Killmer collection

MB Boucher blue and white enameled bird with extra long tail, perched on a branch, signed, **$295.00 – 395.00.** Cheryl Killmer collection

Another creature brooch, this one with dragons, and a scary monkey face, again with genuine look stones and a prong-set imitation pearl, brooch is 2½" wide, and unsigned, **$150.00 – 175.00.** Cheryl Killmer collection

Back view of brooch.

Unsigned French Edwardian period brooch with eight flowerettes with riveted frames and large center rhinestones surrounded by foiled gray prong-set rhinestones, brooch is 3¾" x 1½" with a safety clasp added on the top of the frame for security, **$150.00 – 175.00.** Dinah Taylor collection

Reverse view of brooch.

Wooden bar pin with carved horse head with laced leather and lace reins, a glass eye, 4" long, **$200.00 – 225.00.** Dinah Taylor collection

Matched set of wooden horse head pins, one with leather bridle in maple, one in walnut with a gold bridle, and one in pine with a gold and brown leather bridle, all have glass eyes, 2¾" x 2½", **$75.00 – 95.00 each.** Dinah Taylor collection

This horse is prepared to ride, he is carrying his saddle, 2½" x 2", **$95.00 – 125.00.** Dinah Taylor collection

Wide eyed horse appears to be stretching for the finish line, 2½" x 2", **$55.00 – 75.00.** Dinah Taylor collection

Coro Craft sterling red bow pin with small red rhinestone accents, 2¾" x 2¾", $250.00 – 275.00.
Sherry James collection

This substantial Benedikt pin requires an anchoring undergarment to display to its full potential. It has five pine cone like star bursts surrounding a large red glass center stone, 2¾" in diameter, $50.00 – 75.00.
Frances E. (Jean) Mitchell collection

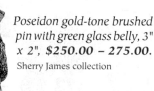

Sarah Coventry spray with brown glass center stone, 2¼" in diameter, $5.00 – 25.00. Frances E. (Jean) Mitchell collection

Poseidon gold-tone brushed pin with green glass belly, 3" x 2", $250.00 – 275.00.
Sherry James collection

Merhorse brushed gold-tone pin with green glass body, 2½" x 2½", $250.00 – 275.00. Sherry James collection

This large flower pin is enameled in red and green with a large imitation pearl center accented with clear rhinestones, 5" long, $25.00 – 45.00. Charles J. (Charlie) Mitchell, Sr. collection

Trifari gold-tone rose blossom is 2¾" with an interesting open petal design, $25.00 – 55.00. Charles J. (Charlie) Mitchell, Sr. collection

Unusual flower bud pin in gold tone, unsigned, 3" long, $10.00 – 25.00. Charles J. (Charlie) Mitchell, Sr. collection

This sweet little flower pin has dark pink satin buds and is 2½" long, $10.00 – 25.00. Frances E. (Jean) Mitchell collection

Who doesn't love a gleeful banana running with his arms akimbo? This unsigned little fellow is 1⅞" tall, $10.00 – 20.00. Frances E. (Jean) Mitchell collection

This delicate yellow flower pin was made in England from bone china, and is a popular tourist's souvenir, 2⅛" in diameter, $20.00 – 45.00. Frances E. (Jean) Mitchell collection

Though small, this pin uses bold red stones to capture attention, 1¾" long, $20.00 – 30.00. Frances E. (Jean) Mitchell collection

Elegant gold-tone bow with rhinestone accents, 2½" x 2½", $25.00 – 45.00. Frances E. (Jean) Mitchell collection

Flower pins continue to make a strong comeback and this large green enameled flower catches the attention quickly with its over-size blossom, 4" tall, $25.00 – 45.00. Charles J. (Charlie) Mitchell, Sr. collection

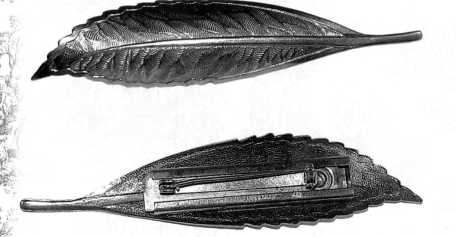

Here is a most unusual pin, at first glance it looks like a simple 3" leaf pin, but it has a big secret. Turn it over, slide the pin mechanism out, and voila! You have a key blank you can use to cut a copy of your house key! How ingenious is that! **$25.00 – 45.00.** Charles J. (Charlie) Mitchell, Sr. collection

Reverse view of pin.

Reverse view showing key blank.

Another view of key blank.

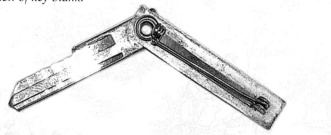

Lovely black and white cameo, 1⅜", my mother was working one day in 1959 when a customer came in wearing this cameo. My mother admired it and the customer took it right off of her dress and gave it to my mother; it is quite lovely, **$75.00 – 150.00.** Frances E. (Jean) Mitchell collection

Adorable little flower pin has an imitation pearl and two genuine green stones, possibly jade, pin is 2¼" tall, **$30.00 – 45.00.** Charles J. (Charlie) Mitchell, Sr. collection

Reverse view of cameo.

Here is an unusual way to share a pin, add it to a vintage post card with matching flowers, this enameled pin is 3" tall, **$25.00 – 45.00.** Charles J. (Charlie) Mitchell, Sr. collection

Here are the famous angel and devil in your shoulder pins from Tortolani, both have blue eyes and are signed with applied plaques. The devil with his forked tail and pitchfork stands 1" tall while the angel stands taller at 1½". This adorable set is **$50.00 – 65.00.** Author collection

This is one of the treasures sent to me by my daddy when he started collecting jewelry for me. This pin even caused a bit of envy when my sister Glynnis spotted it and tried to pilfer it from the package headed my way, but daddy firmly said no, it was for me. And I adore it. It is a red stone flower with all prong-set rhinestones in round, marquise, and emerald shapes, and I believe it is a 1950s design. 2⅞" x 2¼". Though I would never sell, you could find one for yourself for **$75.00 – 95.00.** Author collection

Reverse view of pin.

Classic and elegant ribbon and spray pin with all prong-set clear baguette and marquise rhinestones, unsigned, though very well made, 3" x 2", $55.00 – 65.00. Author collection

Reverse view of pin.

Here is a fun and well made galloping horse with a black eye, red nostril, and fringe tail, he has a brushed finish and is signed "J.J.," 2½" with tail extended, $25.00 – 35.00. J.J. jewelry is quite popular because they made something for everyone.
Author collection

Monet frolicking horse pin with enameled bangs, mane, tail, and hooves, signed "MONET" on back of tail, 3" x 1½", $35.00 – 45.00.
Author collection

This enameled urn fur clip actually holds water and a flower bud or bloom, it is nearly 2" tall, and is unsigned, $95.00 – 125.00. Author collection

A flock of ducks by Marc Labat in silver-toned metal, 2½" x 1¼", signed "Marc LABAT PARIS," $45.00 – 65.00. Author collection

Reverse view of fur clip.

Reverse view of pin with signature.

Wonderfully rendered morning glory enameled pin in pale blue, one of the
HAR flower blossom designs, 1¾" x 1¼",
$45.00 – 65.00. Author collection

Stunning 1940s floral bouquet with colored stamens inside the largest bloom, the two blooms
on either side are riveted on and both
turn, 4" tall, **$125.00 – 150.00.**
Author collection

Matched pair of wrapped candies pins,
one in silver-tone metal, the other in gold
tone, each pin has seven tiny
cabochon accents, and each is
marked on the back "MADE
ITALY." Both have a European trombone clasp, 2¼" x⅞",
$95.00 – 125.00 each. Author
collection

*Reverse view
of pin.*

*Reverse view of
pins showing sig-
nature.*

This Eisenberg pin is marked only with a script "E," it is
1⅞" x 1¼" with prong-set clear rhinestones, **$95.00 –
125.00.** Author collection

*Reverse view
of pin.*

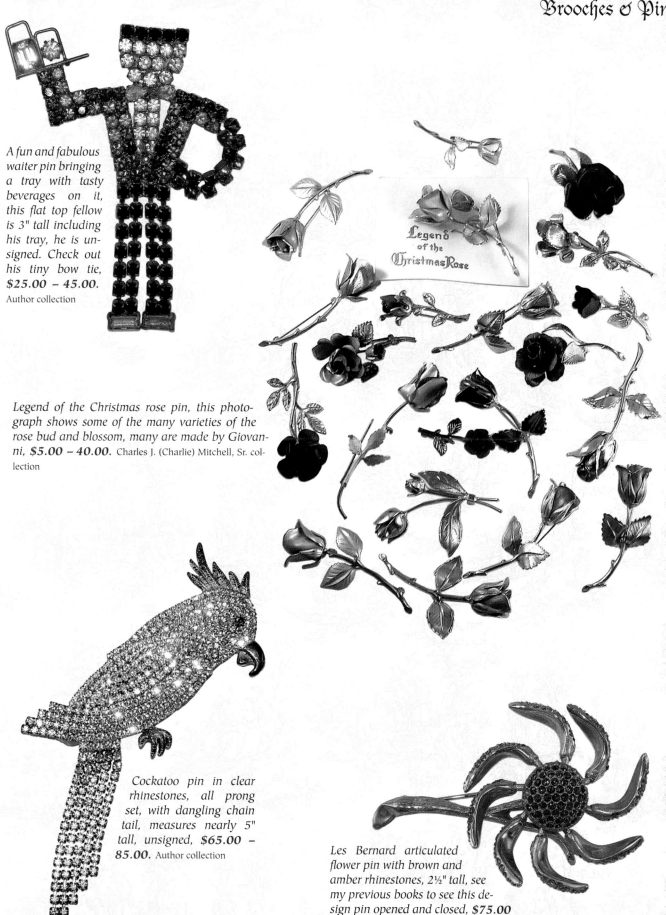

A fun and fabulous waiter pin bringing a tray with tasty beverages on it, this flat top fellow is 3" tall including his tray, he is unsigned. Check out his tiny bow tie, **$25.00 – 45.00.** Author collection

Legend of the Christmas rose pin, this photograph shows some of the many varieties of the rose bud and blossom, many are made by Giovanni, **$5.00 – 40.00.** Charles J. (Charlie) Mitchell, Sr. collection

Cockatoo pin in clear rhinestones, all prong set, with dangling chain tail, measures nearly 5" tall, unsigned, **$65.00 – 85.00.** Author collection

Les Bernard articulated flower pin with brown and amber rhinestones, 2½" tall, see my previous books to see this design pin opened and closed, **$75.00 – 95.00.** Author collection

Brooches & Pins

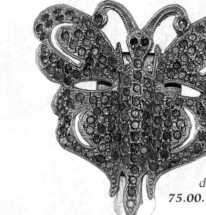

Milk glass and aurora borealis prong-set pin from the 1950s, unsigned, 1½" in diameter, one of the treasures from daddy, **$20.00 – 30.00.** Author collection

Beautifully designed butterfly dress clip from the 1940s, very high quality, 1⅝" x 1⅝", another treasure from daddy, pictures sadly don't do it justice, **$50.00 – 75.00.** Author collection

Very high domed pin with pink, clear, and white givré prong-set rhinestones, unsigned, 1⅞" in diameter, a treasure from daddy, **$55.00 – 75.00.** Author collection

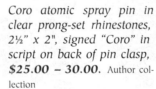

Coro atomic spray pin in clear prong-set rhinestones, 2½" x 2", signed "Coro" in script on back of pin clasp, **$25.00 – 30.00.** Author collection

Gorgeous B. David spray pin in clear prong-set rhinestones, 3" x 1½", a treasure found by my daddy, **$65.00 – 75.00.** Author collection

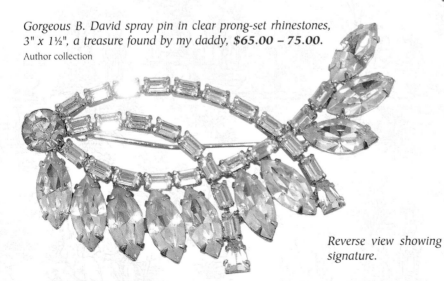

Reverse view showing signature.

Sterling snowflake pin with clear and amber prong-set rhinestones, 2¼" in diameter, center stone is open backed, **$85.00 – 95.00.** Author collection

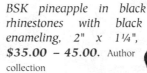

BSK pineapple in black rhinestones with black enameling, 2" x 1¼", **$35.00 – 45.00.** Author collection

This leaf and cultured pearl pin is marked "1/20 12 K G" and "WRE" which is the mark of the W.E. Richards Company from North Attleboro, MA, in business since around 1900. Circle pins were very popular during the 1950s, 1¼" in diameter, **$45.00 – 50.00.** Author collection

The ubiquitous poodle pin, also popular during the 1950s, this one has pale blue rhinestones with a red rhinestone eye, 1¼" x 2", **$15.00 – 25.00.** Author collection

Adorable flamingo pin with glass rhinestones and a pink Lucite body, all stones are prong set, unsigned, 3" x 2¼", **$75.00 – 95.00.** Author collection

Elegant rhinestone flamingo, pink and clear stones, and a green stone eye, and enameled beak, unsigned, 2⅝" x 1¼", **$35.00 – 50.00.** Author collection

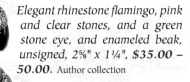

Reverse view of pin.

Pair of fur clips in pink and blue enameling with moonstone cabochons, clips are nearly identical, but only the pink one is marked "Coro." The pink one has metal beads accents while the blue one has rhinestones accents, clips are 2¾" x 2", **$75.00 – 95.00** each. Author collection

Gorgeous bird in flight by Mazer, with red and green baguettes and medium blue oval rhinestones, which are open backed, pin is signed "Mazer," 2¼" x 2", with a depth of over 1", well made and heavy, **$250.00 – 295.00.** Author collection

Reverse view of clips.

Reverse view of pin.

This fur clip with fruit salad stones and clear rhinestone accents is from the Trifari Floraleaf collection, the original ad can be seen in Volume 2 on page 175. The ad says it is pale opalescent moonstone with golden Trifanium, and they were called clip-pins, and originally sold for $25.00 each. Clip-pin has a safety clasp on it and it is 2¼" x 1¼"; it is signed "crown Trifari" and "Pat. Pend," **$155.00 – 175.00.** Author collection

Reverse view of fur clip.

Les Bernard articulated pink flower pin with petals that move in any position from a bud to fully opened, with medium pink, pale pink, and very light pink rhinestones, 3" x 2¼", signed "Les Bernard Inc." and "Pat. Pend.," **$125.00 – 150.00.** Author collection

Florenza cameo pin also has a bale for a pendant, and is signed Florenza on back, 1¾" x 1½₂", it is a genuine shell cameo featuring a lady with a large nose, she is framed with imitation pearls, and the pin has a depth of nearly ½", **$20.00 – 30.00.** Author collection

Reverse view of pin.

If you have any of my books, then you know I love flamingo pins, and the set that has enameling and different colored rhinestone bodies are some of my favorites. This green fellow is from the 1940s, and came in quite a mix of colors. This one has all dark green rhinestones and a red stone eye, he is 3⅛" x 2", unsigned, **$100.00 – 125.00.** Author collection

Pair of pins together, showing size differential.

Now, this little fellow is from the same series, but he is tiny in comparison, he stands 1⅞" x 1¼" and is unsigned. He has enameling and rhinestones and his eye is enameled, **$40.00 – 45.00.** Author collection

This red heart pin is a Claudette design, you can see the pin with matching marked earrings in blue in my first book, the earrings came in a round button design and also a matching heart-shaped design, it has glued-in round rhinestones and red cabochons, it also has a bale to wear as a necklace, 2¼" x 1¾", **$75.00 – 85.00.** Author collection

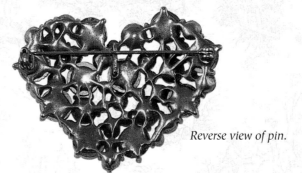

Reverse view of pin.

The following are a series of pins made by Lea Stein out of Paris, France. The trees came in a variety of different colors. Tree pins are 3¼" x 2⅛", and are signed "Lea Stein Paris." Note some of the trees have stars atop of them and some do not, **$125.00 – 130.00** each. All author collection

Red and black tree with multi-colored star topper.

Light green and dark green tree with dark green star topper.

White and silver glitter tree without star topper.

Black and silver tree pin without topper.

Lilac and lavender tree pin without topper.

Reverse view of lilac and lavender pin, note signature on pin clasp.

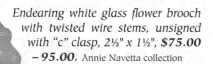

Endearing white glass flower brooch with twisted wire stems, unsigned with "c" clasp, 2½" x 1½", *$75.00 – 95.00.* Annie Navetta collection

Unusual damascene with jade cabochons flower spray, marked "Spain," 2⅓" x 1½", *$35.00 – 45.00.* Annie Navetta collection

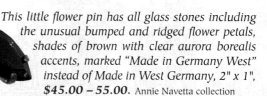

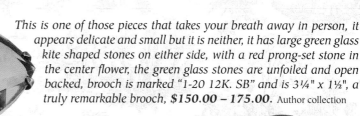

This little flower pin has all glass stones including the unusual bumped and ridged flower petals, shades of brown with clear aurora borealis accents, marked "Made in Germany West" instead of Made in West Germany, 2" x 1", *$45.00 – 55.00.* Annie Navetta collection

This is one of those pieces that takes your breath away in person, it appears delicate and small but it is neither, it has large green glass kite shaped stones on either side, with a red prong-set stone in the center flower, the green glass stones are unfoiled and open backed, brooch is marked "1-20 12K. SB" and is 3¼" x 1½", a truly remarkable brooch, *$150.00 – 175.00.* Author collection

Reverse view of brooch.

Wonderful blue moonstone basket pin, unsigned but could be Coro with 10 star sapphire look moonstone cabochons, which are all open backed, 2¼" x 2¼", *$165.00 – 185.00.* Author collection

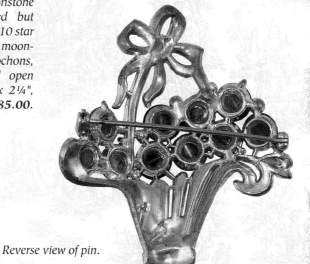

Reverse view of pin.

157

Brooches & Pins

This pin is one of the designs of unplated prong-set pins currently being offered from sellers in the Czech Republic. Most of these pins are unsigned, though a few have marks such as Husar, Design By Romi, Husar D, and Lilien. Most are large size designs, and they are currently quite popular with collectors. This horse pin with various types, colors, and sizes of rhinestones is 3¼" wide and nearly 3¼" tall, with a dangling rhinestone chain tail. All stones are prong set. These pins are said to be vintage but some collectors believe that old blanks are being set with rhinestones to be offered on today's market. Collectors should be careful not to wear these pins on anything that allows the unplated backs to come into contact with bare skin. That said, I love these pins, they appeal to my desire for oversized jewelry. Values for most should be around **$15.00 – 30.00** but some designs, such as a 4½" wasp are selling for prices over $75.00. Horse pin **$20.00 – 25.00.** Author collection

Reverse view of horse pin, note some stones are open backed.

Ballerina from the Czech Republic, all stones are prong set, skirt has black chatons and jade green oval cabochons, 4" x 2⅞", **$20.00 – 25.00.** Author collection

Reverse view of ballerina pin.

This particular pin is one reason collectors love these designs, it is a geisha wearing a kimono and carrying a fan, wearing hair combs. Her kimono is made from rhinestone chain that dangles, she has a signature plaque reading "Design by Romi," 4" x 2½", **$20.00 – 25.00.** Author collection

Reverse view showing signature plaque.

Gold-tone leaf by BSK with dark blue rhinestones pavéd in half of furled leaf, 2" x 1⅝", **$45.00 – 55.00.** Author collection

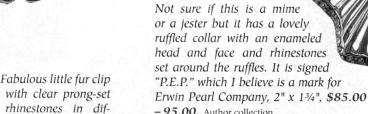

Reverse view showing open setting between rhinestones.

Not sure if this is a mime or a jester but it has a lovely ruffled collar with an enameled head and face and rhinestones set around the ruffles. It is signed "P.E.P." which I believe is a mark for Erwin Pearl Company, 2" x 1¾", **$85.00 – 95.00.** Author collection

Fabulous little fur clip with clear prong-set rhinestones in different shapes, signed "Weiss," 1¼" x ¾", **$40.00 – 45.00.** Author collection

Reverse view of fur clip showing signature.

Reverse view of pin.

A single bee from the Coro queen bee duette, this little bee has red rhinestone eyes, enameling, and rhinestone accents across its body, it is unsigned, 1¾" x 1", **$35.00 – 55.00.** Author collection

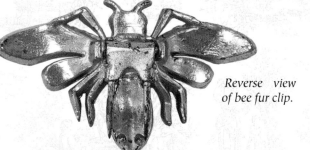

Reverse view of bee fur clip.

This dainty butterfly stick pin is made from pieces of mother of pearl, and though unsigned, it has the clutch pin characteristic of Miriam Haskell stick pins; butterfly is 1¼" wide, **$35.00 – 45.00.** Author collection

Reverse view of butterfly.

Brooches & Pins

Reverse view of brooch.

This pin has all of the characteristics of a Mazer design, with the large prong-set rhinestone flourish and rhinestone accented ribbon, attached with two rivets, but it is unsigned. Brooch is 3½" x 2", very heavy, and the red stones are unfoiled and open backed, **$95.00 – 125.00.** Author collection

This pin combines all of the best of Les Bernard, rhinestones and marcasites which are mounted upside down, and a cultured pearl in the center, it is signed and 1½" x 1½", **$65.00 – 75.00.** Author collection

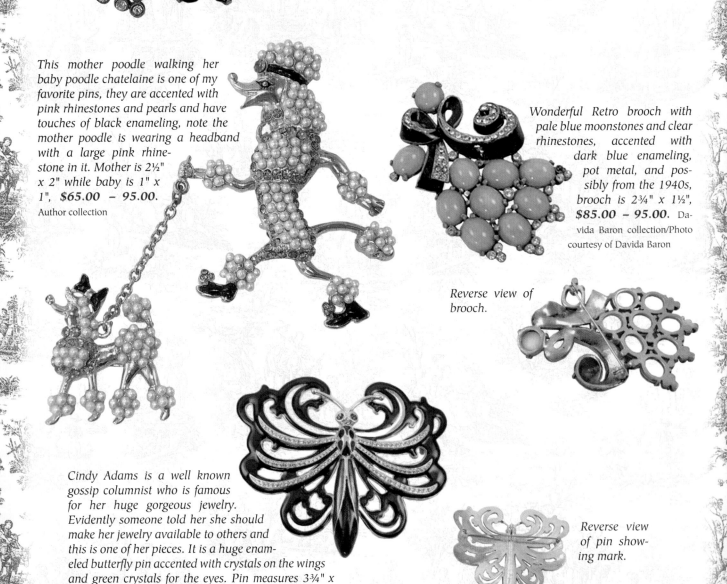

This mother poodle walking her baby poodle chatelaine is one of my favorite pins, they are accented with pink rhinestones and pearls and have touches of black enameling, note the mother poodle is wearing a headband with a large pink rhinestone in it. Mother is 2½" x 2" while baby is 1" x 1", **$65.00 – 95.00.** Author collection

Wonderful Retro brooch with pale blue moonstones and clear rhinestones, accented with dark blue enameling, pot metal, and possibly from the 1940s, brooch is 2¾" x 1½", **$85.00 – 95.00.** Davida Baron collection/Photo courtesy of Davida Baron

Reverse view of brooch.

Cindy Adams is a well known gossip columnist who is famous for her huge gorgeous jewelry. Evidently someone told her she should make her jewelry available to others and this is one of her pieces. It is a huge enameled butterfly pin accented with crystals on the wings and green crystals for the eyes. Pin measures 3¾" x 3" and is signed on the back "Cindy Adams," **$85.00 – 95.00.** Davida Baron collection/Photo courtesy of Davida Baron

Reverse view of pin showing mark.

160

Ciner has been in business for over 100 years creating high-end jewelry, their quality has never been compromised, evidenced by this huge bow pin encrusted with clear rhinestones, it is 3½" x 1½" and is signed on the back, **$125.00 – 145.00.** Davida Baron collection/Photo courtesy of Davida Baron

Reverse view of Ciner pin showing Florentine finish and signature.

Sterling Coro Craft bird brooch with enameling and clear rhinestones, brooch is over sized at 4" x 2¾", signed on the back, a rarely seen design, **$250.00 – 295.00.** Davida Baron collection/ Photo courtesy of Davida Baron

This three-dimensional brooch design screams Czech and early 1930s, though it is unsigned. The blue glass cabochon is surrounded by rhinestones separated by curly dividers of solid brass with filigree inside. Brooch is 2¾" in diameter with a solid brass back, **$200.00 – 250.00.** Davida Baron collection/Photo courtesy of Davida Baron

Reverse view of brooch showing signature.

Reverse view of brooch.

Czech brooch with bezel-set glass stones in pink, green, blue, citrine, and aqua, with heavy curly open filigree, copied later by famous designers, unsigned pin is 2½" in diameter, **$150.00 – 175.00.** Davida Baron collection/Photo courtesy of Davida Baron

This crown pin with orange glass stones is signed "The Show Must Go On" which is the signature of David Mandel's company; it is an abstract modernist crown with glass stones and a silver-tone metal back. Design is from the 1990s, and pin is 2¾" x 2¾", **$125.00 – 150.00.** Davida Baron collection/Photo courtesy of Davida Baron

Reverse view showing filigree backing.

Reverse view showing signature.

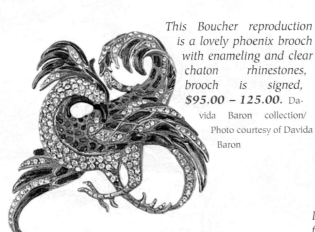

This Boucher reproduction is a lovely phoenix brooch with enameling and clear chaton rhinestones, brooch is signed, **$95.00 – 125.00.** Davida Baron collection/Photo courtesy of Davida Baron

Reverse view of brooch.

Lovely enameled tulip pin from the 1930s, with clear rhinestone accents. Unsigned pin is pot metal and is 3¼" x 2¾", **$65.00 – 95.00.** Davida Baron collection/Photo courtesy of Davida Baron

Cornucopia pin looks to be Czech in origin and from the 1930s, the back has an open filigree design, and is unsigned. Front is very dimensional with amethyst glass stones, pin is 3¼" x 2¼", **$85.00 – 95.00.** Davida Baron collection/Photo courtesy of Davida Baron

Reverse view of brooch.

This pin is not signed but it has the characteristics of a Regency design, with blue and green rhinestones, all prong set, and foiled, many with an open back, brooch is 3¾" in diameter. It also has a bale attached to allow it to be worn as a pendant, **$125.00 – 165.00.** Davida Baron collection/Photo courtesy of Davida Baron

Beautiful enameled and rhinestone bird pin looks to be a Boucher design but it is unsigned, made of pot metal and likely a 1950s design, **$50.00 – 65.00.** Davida Baron collection/Photo courtesy of Davida Baron

Reverse view of pin.

Reverse view of pin.

Floral bouquet brooch with ribbon is unsigned but looks like a Mazer design, it has clear rhinestones and beautiful amethyst stone and an amethyst cabochon, 4⅞" x 3¾", **$225.00 – 250.00.** Davida Baron collection/ Photo courtesy of Davida Baron

Reverse view of brooch.

Green and clear Art Deco look paste brooch, possibly French, and absolutely gorgeous. Brooch is 3" x 2" and is unsigned, **$150.00 – 185.00.** Davida Baron collection/Photo courtesy of Davida Baron

This paste brooch with green glass leaves is likely French in origin and from the 1930s. It is unsigned, and made of pot metal and the leaves are wired onto the brooch, 3¾" x 2½", **$175.00 – 195.00.** Davida Baron collection/ Photo courtesy of Davida Baron

Reverse view of brooch.

Fred Block enamel and rhinestone fur clip with prong-set stones, clip is signed on the back, and has the look of a Vogue design. Fur clip is nearly 2¾" in diameter, **$175.00 – 250.00.** Davida Baron collection/Photo courtesy of Davida Baron

Did you ever see vintage belt buckles and wish you could wear them as a brooch? This one has been put together to be worn as a brooch, it has an Art Deco look with an openwork design and long blue poured glass stones. Brooch has two clasps, allowing it to be worn either sideways or upwards, 4¾" x 2½", **$150.00 – 175.00.** Davida Baron collection/Photo courtesy of Davida Baron

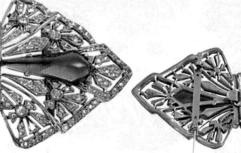

Reverse view showing two pin clasps.

Reverse view of brooch.

This is a great example of the vase brooches so popular in the 1930s. It is not signed but should have been, as it has wonderful workmanship. There is an antique gold-tone metal stand holding a stunning blue faceted glass vase and filled with enameled flowers accented with rhinestones, brooch is 2½" x 2¾", **$125.00 – 175.00.** Davida Baron collection/Photo courtesy of Davida Baron

Unsigned Vogue flower brooch with prong-set stones in clear and green, wires can be manipulated to make brooch three dimensional, brooch is 4" x 2½", **$100.00 – 150.00.** Davida Baron collection/Photo courtesy of Davida Baron

Reverse view of brooch.

Hattie Carnegie star brooch with large green glass stone and purple and amber cabochons in a pewter metal color, 4" in diameter, **$125.00 – 150.00.** Davida Baron collection/Photo courtesy of Davida Baron

Reverse view of brooch.

Stunning fur clip filled with gorgeous rhinestones in a great color combination, note flower design in center of clip, 3" x 2¼", **$150.00 – 175.00.** Davida Baron collection/Photo courtesy of Davida Baron

Reverse view of fur clip showing foiled stones and open back.

Floral dress clip with prong-set rhinestones and imitation pearls, also prong set, unsigned, clip is 3" x 2⅛", **$75.00 – 85.00.** Davida Baron collection/ Photo courtesy of Davida Baron

Dazzling unsigned Vogue brooch in green and pink rhinestones, prong set, with clear accents, a stylized vase design, 3½" x 3¼", **$500.00 – 525.00.** Davida Baron collection/Photo courtesy of Davida Baron

Reverse view of brooch.

Enchanting heart-shaped unsigned Vogue brooch with prong-set red and clear rhinestones, some of the center stones are on wires allowing them to be manipulated to give this brooch a three dimensional look, 2¾" x 2⅛", **$200.00 – 225.00.** Davida Baron collection/Photo courtesy of Davida Baron

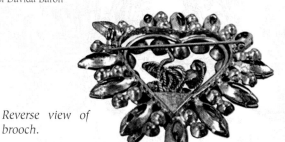

Reverse view of brooch.

Modernistic cornucopia brooch by Robert Sorrell, filled with colorful rhinestones and lined with clear rhinestones, 4¼" x 4", **$400.00 – 450.00.** Davida Baron collection/Photo courtesy of Davida Baron

Reverse view of brooch.

This striking blue Larry Vrba spider brooch is huge, measuring 5¾" x 3½", it is designed to move as you move, signed "Lawrence Vrba," **$350.00 – 395.00.** Davida Baron collection/Photo courtesy of Davida Baron

Unsigned Vogue heart flower bouquet with a rhinestone heart anchoring a spray of stylized flowers, with wires you can manipulate to give it a three-dimensional look, 3¾" x 2¼", **$75.00 – 125.00.** Davida Baron collection/Photo courtesy of Davida Baron

Reverse view of brooch.

165

Palette brooch with prong-set rhinestones in pinks and blues with green enameling, unsigned but looks like a Vogue design, 3¼" x 2", $125.00 – 155.00. Davida Baron collection/ Photo courtesy of Davida Baron

Floral spray in a stylized vase or cornucopia, flowers are connected to wires you can move to make the brooch three dimensional, unsigned but very Vogue-like in design, 3¾" x 2¼", $125.00 – 155.00. Davida Baron collection/Photo courtesy of Davida Baron

Reverse view of brooch.

Reverse view of brooch.

Delicate looking heart bouquet by Vogue with prong-set stones in clear, green, purple, and pink, signed "Vogue," 4¼" x 2¼" with moveable wires, $175.00 – 195.00. Davida Baron collection/Photo courtesy of Davida Baron

Reverse view of brooch showing signature.

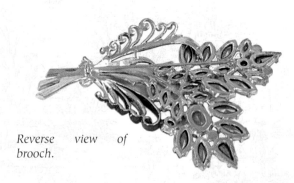

Reverse view of brooch.

Large floral spray in shades of blue made by Fenichel, brooch has large prong-set stones which are open backed accented with clear rhinestones. Brooch is signed "Fenichel," and is 4¼" x 2¾", $125.00 – 165.00. Davida Baron collection/Photo courtesy of Davida Baron

Reverse view showing signature.

Large pot-metal brooch likely made in the 1950s and signed "Kandell & Marcus," it is a leafy flower spray set with multicolored rhinestones, 4¼" x 3", **$85.00 – 95.00.** Davida Baron collection/Photo courtesy of Davida Baron

View showing mark.

Reverse view of brooch.

This pin by Pomerantz could be either an urn or a vase, filled with prong-set red and purple rhinestones, accented with clear stones, and signed "Pomerantz Inc. NY," probably dating to the 1930s, 3" x 2", **$125.00 – 150.00.** Davida Baron collection/Photo courtesy of Davida Baron

Reverse view showing signature.

Reverse view of fur clip.

Trifari fur clip with gorgeous blue baguettes flowing down to red and pink oval glass stones, prong set, unfoiled and open backed, signed with the "crown Trifari." Brooch is 3" x 1½", **$200.00 – 250.00.** Davida Baron collection/Photo courtesy of Davida Baron

Another fabulous floral vase brooch filled with heart-shaped and hexagon glass stones, vase base is an amethyst glass stone. Though unsigned, this could be a De Rosa design, it is 3" x 3", and probably dates to the early 1940s, **$350.00 – 395.00.** Davida Baron collection/Photo courtesy of Davida Baron

Reverse view of brooch.

167

Enameled Coro bird in wonderful condition, the bird is sitting on an enameled branch with a flower extending towards its tail, signed "Coro" in script, 3½" x 2½", **$95.00 – 125.00.** Davida Baron collection/Photo courtesy of Davida Baron

Reverse view of bird pin.

Lovely Czech pin/pendant from the 1930s, with a beautiful mixture of pastel stones, and a double chain holding a drop with filigreed stones, 3½" x 2¼", **$125.00 – 165.00.** Davida Baron collection/Photo courtesy of Davida Baron

Kenneth Jay Lane pin/pendant with a regal look with pink and green glass stones and imitation pearls, the crown at the top has pink moonstone cabochons on either side of an emerald green cabochon, anchoring the design with dangling glass beads, signed "KJL," 3" x 2", **$175.00 – 195.00.** Davida Baron collection/ Photo courtesy of Davida Baron

Reverse view showing signature.

Lovely wheat flower brooch with the "S" in a star mark, sometimes seen with Made in USA, and found on designs patented by Jose Rodriguez, but unknown who exactly this company is, yet. This brooch has pink, clear, and blue rhinestones, and the large pink stones are unfoiled and open backed, 4" x 2¾", **$125.00 – 165.00.** Davida Baron collection/Photo courtesy of Davida Baron

Reverse view of brooch, note star with "S" mark near top behind clasp.

Close up of mark.

Dress clip with a heart shape and clear and ruby red rhinestones, beautiful design with some of the stones being foiled and open backed, 3" x 2", **$100.00 – 125.00.** Davida Baron collection/ Photo courtesy of Davida Baron

Beautiful old pot-metal brooch with the look of Mazer, Coro, or even Trifari, with pale blue moonstone cabochons, in a lovely flower bouquet, accented with clear rhinestones, unsigned, 3⅛" x 2¾", **$150.00 – 165.00.** Davida Baron collection/Photo courtesy of Davida Baron

Reverse view of dress clip.

Reverse view of brooch.

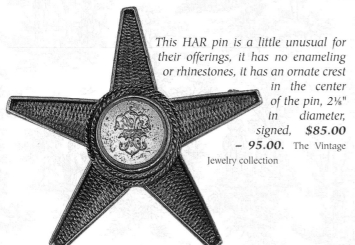

This HAR pin is a little unusual for their offerings, it has no enameling or rhinestones, it has an ornate crest in the center of the pin, 2⅛" in diameter, signed, **$85.00 – 95.00.** The Vintage Jewelry collection

Reverse view showing signature.

Great flower pin by Vendôme with three blooms filled with aurora borealis blue rhinestones, signed on back, 2¼" x 1½", **$140.00 – 165.00.** The Vintage Jewelry collection

Reverse view of pin.

169

Reverse view of pin.

Deja bird in flight pin, signed "Deja," enameled with rhinestone accents, 1¼" x 2", **$250.00 – 295.00.** The Vintage Jewelry collection

Beautiful heart-shaped brooch from West Germany, with blue and green rhinestones, all prong set, **$125.00 – 145.00.** The Vintage Jewelry collection

West German brooch with amber colored stones and cabochons, accented with imitation pearls and imitation tiger eye stones, signed, filigree back, 2¼" in diameter, **$95.00 – 125.00.** The Vintage Jewelry collection

Reverse view showing filigree back.

Reverse view showing signature.

Weiss flower pin with three blooms filled with prong-set blue rhinestones, signed, jewelry is being produced in mass quantities today with the Weiss signature, most prolific are butterflies and Christmas tree pins, and the value of Weiss is decreasing with the reproductions. This pin is 2½" x 1¼", **$65.00 – 95.00.** The Vintage Jewelry collection

Pair of fruit salad scatter pins with carved glass fruit stones in pastel shades, with clear rhinestone accents, unsigned, 1⅛" x ¾", **$40.00 – 55.00 for the pair.** Author collection

Reverse view of scatter pins.

Wonderful rendition of enameled plums with leaves and rhinestone accents, this pin is unsigned but is identical to the line of fruit and vegetable jewelry made by Reja, with incredible detailing of the enamel and the rhinestones set under the leaf, pin is 2¾" x 1½", extremely well made, if Reja, **$295.00 – 395.00,** as an unattributed great design, **$95.00 – 125.00.** Author collection

Fabulous design by Carolee of a cat in sunglasses playing the saxophone, signed "CAROLEE," with enameling and rhinestones, note rhinestone collar, 1⅞" x 1⅜", **$95.00 – 145.00.** Author collection

Ceramic cat pin by Ruby Z in black and white with amber eyes, signed with a black stamp, 3¼" x 2", **$25.00 – 35.00.** Author collection

Napier brushed gold-tone cherries dangling from a branch, signed, 2¼" x 1⅞", three-dimensional cherries are hollow but thick walled, **$35.00 – 55.00.** Author collection

Brooches & Pins

Ceramic Flying Colors black and white cat with green eyes, a pink nose, and pink ears, signed "Flying Colors" with a black stamp, 1¾" x 1¼", **$10.00 – 20.00.** Author collection

Floral bouquet pin is filled with blooms of different colored aurora borealis stones, in pink, reds, and blues, unsigned, 3" x 2⅓", one of daddy's finds, **$35.00 – 65.00.** Author collection

Running giraffe pin looks like a Boucher design, pin is marked "A1754," enameled with clear rhinestones and a green rhinestone eye, 2" x 2", **$25.00 – 55.00.** Author collection

Bar pin with red and clear rhinestones, unsigned, 2¾" x ⅝", **$10.00 – 20.00.** Author collection

Trifari camilla pin with milk glass petals that look like poured glass, signed "crown Trifari," 2¼" in diameter, from 1952, shown in a Mother's Day ad, **$35.00 – 55.00.** Author collection

Circle pin with all prong-set clear and red rhinestones, note red stones have 10 prongs each, 1⅛" in diameter, **$10.00 – 20.00.** Author collection

Lavender flowers in very light weight plastic with prong-set purple stones, pot metal, signed with the "S" in a star mark and "Made in USA," 4" x 2½", **$10.00 – 25.00.** Author collection

Elzac ceramic lady with chenille sequined bodice and hat, 4" tall, **$85.00 – 165.00.** Kim Paff collection/Photo courtesy of www.kimsvintage.com

Pretty blue and green enameled flower pin with lady bug alighting on one petal, unsigned, 3½" x 1¾", **$10.00 – 25.00.** Author collection

Elzac lady with crocheted bonnet and silk taffeta bow, she is on a wooden back, and is 3¾" tall, **$85.00 – 165.00.** Kim Paff collection/Photo courtesy of www.kimsvintage.com

Spectacular green rhinestone bird with red eye brooch, he is turning his head making him three dimensional, unsigned pot metal, 4" x 3¾" and his head is raised 1¼", **$145.00 – 165.00.** Kim Paff collection/Photo courtesy of www. kimsvintage.com

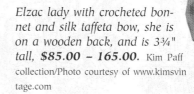

Matched set of Matisse Renoir enameled copper artist's palette brooches in a variety of colors, 4" long, all signed, **$55.00 – 75.00** *each.* Kim Paff collection/Photo courtesy of www.kimsvintage.com

Rare sterling flower bouquet pin by Guglielmo Cini, an Italian jeweler that moved to the United States in the early 1920s, visit www.cinijewelry.com for more information. Pin is signed "Giglielmo Cini Sterling," and is 3⅛" x 2¼", **$95.00 – 155.00.** Author collection

Close up of signature.

Reverse view of pin.

Earrings

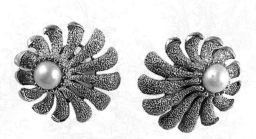

Stylish Trifari clip earrings with imitation pearl centers in silver tone, 1" in diameter, **$20.00 – 35.00.** Frances E. (Jean) Mitchell collection

Miriam Haskell earrings in black with clear rhinestones, 1¼" square, **$135.00 – 165.00.** Cheryl Killmer collection

Large gold-tone hoop earrings with rhinestone flower tops, signed "Deanna Hamro," **$125.00 – 175.00.** Cheryl Killmer collection

William de Lillo enormous hoop earrings with white and black glass, 3½" x 2¾", **$300.00 – 325.00.** Judy Miller collection

Beautiful pink art glass earrings with rhinestone accents by Jomaz, both earrings are signed and have the pat. number on them, 1¼" in diameter, **$50.00 – 65.00.** Author collection

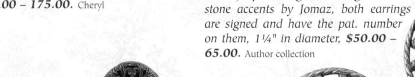

Miriam Haskell clip earrings are 2½" long, **$200.00 – 225.00.** Judy Miller collection

Reverse view of earrings.

174

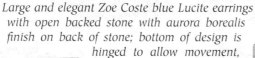

Large and elegant Zoe Coste blue Lucite earrings with open backed stone with aurora borealis finish on back of stone; bottom of design is hinged to allow movement, 2¼" x 1", only one earring is signed "Zoe Coste Made in France." **$75.00 – 95.00.** Author collection

Reverse view of earrings.

Very well made sky blue rhinestone earrings, all stones are open backed, foiled, and prong set, though unsigned, 1" in diameter, **$25.00 – 30.00.** Author collection

Another well made pair of earrings with glass and Lucite stones, all are prong set and the tear-drop shaped stones are open backed, I believe this was originally a pair of pierced earrings that have been converted, earrings are 1" in diameter, **$20.00 – 25.00.** Author collection

Reverse view of earrings.

This wildly colorful pair of earrings is from David Mandel for "The Show Must Go On," and each earring is marked with the applied plaque, earrings are 1½" tall and all stones are prong set, with the celery green stone being open backed, **$50.00 – 65.00.** Author collection

Reverse view of earrings.

Mazer Bros. earrings in gold tone with dark green and clear rhinestones, beautiful design, both earrings are signed, 1" tall, **$95.00 – 125.00.** Author collection

I believe these are D&E Juliana earrings but I have not run them through the verification process yet. They have gorgeous stones including dark green marquise stones which have open backs and are unfoiled, the round green stone is also unfoiled and open backed, 1⅛" tall, **$25.00 – 45.00.** Author collection

Reverse view of earrings.

Earrings

This is one fabulous and eye-catching pair of earrings by Zoe Coste, they have huge red Lucite round cabochons and they came with ear cushions, making them very comfortable to wear despite their size. Both earrings are signed "Zoe Coste Made in France," 2¼" x 1⅜", **$75.00 – 95.00.** Author collection

Reverse view of earrings.

Volupté pale green poured glass earrings with green rhinestone accent, this is a rare design from Volupté, 1⅜" x 1¼", both are signed, **$95.00 – 125.00.** Author collection

These earrings are gorgeous in person, they have prong-set demi lune stones and large baguettes, I have seen a Trifari necklace that is a perfect match to these earrings, though they are unmarked, 1¼" x ¾", **$25.00 – 45.00.** Author collection

Reverse view of earrings.

Reverse view of earrings.

These earrings were sold to me as unsigned, because the Jomaz signature is so faint you can't read it without magnification, earrings are 2" long and are screw on clips, **$55.00 – 65.00.** Author collection

Beautifully designed shades of blue earrings with all prong-set stones, including two large cabochons, one of which has an aurora borealis finish, unsigned, 1⅛" x 1", **$35.00 – 55.00.** Author collection

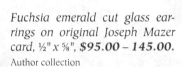

Fuchsia emerald cut glass earrings on original Joseph Mazer card, ½" x ⅝", **$95.00 – 145.00.** Author collection

Coro earrings with molded flower buds each holding a single rhinestone, both signed "Coro," 1⅜" tall, **$10.00 – 20.00.** Author collection

Kunio Matsumoto for Trifari enameled goldtone earrings, signed, **$45.00 – 65.00.** Kim Paff collection/Photo courtesy of www.kimsvintage.com

Rings & Things

Florenza high domed Renaissance style ring with a ⁷⁄₁₆" forest green cabochon center stone surrounded by a twisted rope design and accented with clear and forest green rhinestones, adjustable, **$45.00 – 55.00.** Cheryl Killmer collection

Sophisticated sterling eight carat quartz ring from the late 1970s to early 1980s, **$195.00 – 225.00.**
Laney Ortega collection

Dazzling green and red Christmas napkin rings with enormous cabochon stones, **$95.00 – 115.00.**
Cheryl Killmer collection

Vendôme adjustable ring from 1969 has what looks like prong-set dark blue marquise rhinestones, but they are actually glued, glued-in ruby red stones, and a turquoise blue cabochon, ring adjusts from about a size 5½ to an 8 with a squared off shank. The dome of the ring sits very high, over ½", signed on back of ring, **$65.00 – 95.00.** Author collection

View showing square shank.

Side view of ring.

Vendôme ring with pink enameling, which has suffered some flaking, ring adjusts from a size 5 to an 8, and has a high dome nearly ½" tall, signed, **$25.00 – 30.00; $45.00 – 55.00** in perfect condition.
Author collection

Here is a classic Vendôme design ring with a large emerald cut stone, this design ring came in a variety of colors, and is very popular with collectors, adjustable from size 5 to 8, stone is nearly ¾" x ½", **$45.00 – 75.00.** Author collection

177

This ring is part of the bold designs from *The House of de Lillo*, and is adjustable with a rope design open shank, star is 1½" in diameter, very rare, **$100.00 – 125.00**. Author collection

Reverse view showing signature.

Side view showing shank.

Sterling silver ring with blue sapphires, beautiful design, size 8, **$40.00 – 50.00**. Author collection

Great rhinestone ring of a small tailed creature, could be a mouse, the slightly adjustable shank goes to size 10, I believe this ring was designed to wear on the index finger because of its large design and size, back is unplated, smaller stones are glass, large center stone is Lucite, mouse is 2¼" tall, **$10.00 – 20.00**. Author collection

Leaping frog ring in green with clear Lucite belly, other stones are glass, like the ring at left, this one is large with a large shank, frog is 1¾" tall, ring is unplated, **$10.00 – 20.00**. Author collection

Quacking duck ring, has large size 10 shank and all glass stones, duck is 1⅓" wide, like the other two Czech rings, this one has all prong-set stones, **$10.00 – 20.00**. Author collection

Large lavender design ring from Betsy Johnson, with Lucite center stone, other stones are glass, size 8, metal looks like rose gold, from 2007, **$45.00 – 65.00**. Author collection

Set of rings from Suzanne Bjontegard, all size 8, with colored and clear rhinestones, set is **$45.00 – 55.00**. Author collection

Set of rings from Suzanne Bjontegard, all size 6, with channel-set stones going all the way around, set is **$40.00 – 50.00**. Author collection

Adjustable ring with large amethyst glass stone, shank opens on side, adjusts to at least an 8, $20.00 – 25.00. Author collection

Lovely pastel Hollycraft adjustable ring, signed "Hollycraft" and "COPR. 1957," in gold tone, wide etched and enameled band, $50.00 – 75.00. Annie Navetta collection

Jomaz with imitation turquoise stone, size 6, $45.00 – 75.00. The Vintage Jewelry collection

Movado ladies purse watch in enamel and sterling, from 1938, watch is signed, and when you open and close it, the winding mechanism activates to wind the watch, this one is in perfect working condition, 3" x 1" open and 1" x 2" closed, $1,100.00 – 1,250.00. The Vintage Jewelry collection

View showing watch closed.

Whiting & Davis mother of pearl and sterling adjustable ring, $55.00 – 75.00. The Vintage Jewelry collection

Buster Brown belt buckle with Buster Brown doing different activities around the frame of the buckle, signed "Pat. Pend." and "Feb. 7 11," 2¼" x 2¾", $125.00 – 135.00. The Vintage Jewelry collection

Reverse view of buckle.

Gorgeous enameled mesh bag with bluebird surrounded by blue flowers, signed inside "Whiting & D," 4¾" tall including clasp and 2⅛" wide, $250.00 – 350.00. The Vintage Jewelry collection

Stand up Czech tree with foiled and unfoiled glass stones, signed "Lilien" and "Czech," 4½" x 3", I am thinking of adding a pin back and wearing it as a Christmas tree pin, **$35.00 – 45.00.** Author collection

Reverse view of ornament.

Lilly Daché hand holding a magnifying glass, hand is adorned with a bracelet and a ring, signed, 3½" x 2" and magnifying glass is another 2", **$125.00 – 175.00.** Kim Paff collection/Photo courtesy of www. kimsvintage.com

Great set of changeable stone rings from Trifari, set has one ring and six different cabochon stones that can be changed for a different look to match your outfit. Cabochons come in white, lapis blue, turquoise blue, red with black lines, tortoise shell, and green turquoise. Cage of ring pops open to allow stones to be changed, **$75.00 – 125.00.** Author collection

Close-up of ring with clasp popped to show how it opens.

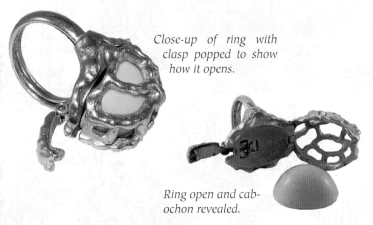

Ring open and cabochon revealed.

Vendôme interchangeable ring set with gold-tone ring that holds different colored balls, sort of like marbles, including an imitation pearl, one that looks like lapis, one that looks like malachite, one that looks amber, and one that is gold tone. This set comes in its original box. Ring is a size 7, **$45.00 – 95.00.** Author collection

Contemporary Jewelry

Designer Dinah Hoyt Taylor is a horse lover who recently began designing jewelry. Most of her designs are taken from nature and she puts her unique spin on her jewelry. Taylor's family started a large commercial winery in 1860 in New York State and they still produce fine varietal wines and champagnes even today, providing further inspiration for Taylor.

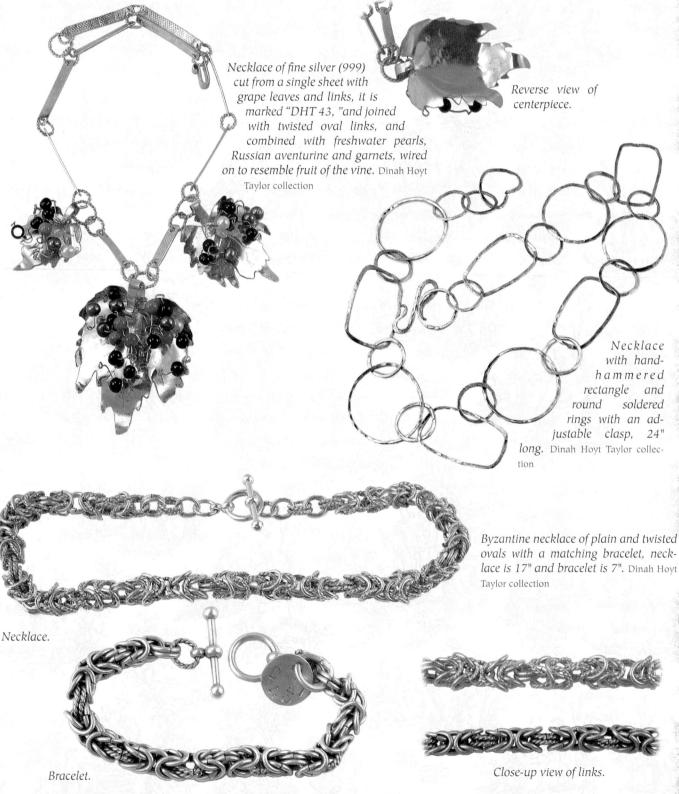

Necklace of fine silver (999) cut from a single sheet with grape leaves and links, it is marked "DHT 43,"and joined with twisted oval links, and combined with freshwater pearls, Russian aventurine and garnets, wired on to resemble fruit of the vine. Dinah Hoyt Taylor collection

Reverse view of centerpiece.

Necklace with hand-hammered rectangle and round soldered rings with an adjustable clasp, 24" long. Dinah Hoyt Taylor collection

Byzantine necklace of plain and twisted ovals with a matching bracelet, necklace is 17" and bracelet is 7". Dinah Hoyt Taylor collection

Necklace.

Bracelet.

Close-up view of links.

Three-strand necklace with coral, rock crystal, amber, and turquoise with sterling, domed squares, 1" diamond shapes, and 1" matching earrings. Dinah Hoyt Taylor collection

This free-form cuff bracelet is named Katrina Waves and is copper textured and formed into the cuff with Czech glass flowers and leaves, it measures 7" x 1½". Cynthia Fore Miller collection

Another free-form bracelet named Summer Honeybees, this large formed and textured cuff with wired glass "bee" beads is 2½" wide.
Dinah Hoyt Taylor collection

Liz Nania rhinestone dragons, contemporary designer from Boston using vintage stones, **$285.00 – 350.00**.

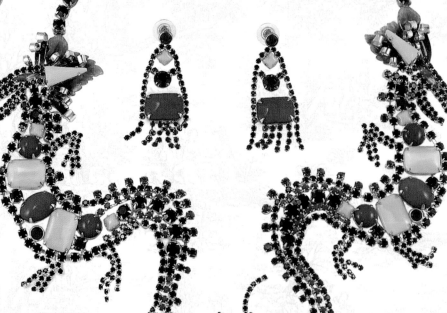

These earrings are from the Kenneth Jay Lane Couture Collection and have safety catches for pierced ears, each is signed "KJL" and they are 1½" long. **$30.00 – 45.00.** They were purchased in 2006. Author collection

These stunning Lucite earrings are also from the Kenneth Jay Lane Couture Collection, they were purchased around 2003 at a Dillards department store. They look like jelly bellies, and both have signatures on the back. They even came with attached cushions, 1¼" tall, **$65.00 – 75.00.** Author collection

This is Madame Ant, a design by Bettina and Michelle Von Walhof and she is one of my all time favorite pins, something about her just appeals to me and she seems to say, "I go with all of your outfits." I do wear her more frequently than any other pin in my collection. If you could see her in person, you would notice her large smile, which doesn't show up in photos. Madame Ant stands 4¼" tall and her head is on a spring, she is 2½" wide. I was wearing her one day when someone said, "your little doll pin is on sideways." I said, "thank you, she is an ant? In a dress?" and the lady replied, "then that is why she is so skinny!" You can find her at the Von Walhof Ruby Lane shop online at rubylane.com, **$95.00 – 100.00.** Author collection

Enameled don-lin Western-themed articulated pin with sheriff's badge, boot, coiled rope, pistol, and spur star, 3½" tall, signed "DON-LIN" and on a card saying "Donald Richard's by don-lin," **$30.00 – 40.00.** Author collection

Suzanne Bjontegard watch with mother of pearl face and aurora borealis rhinestones, watch face and back have the SB mark, **$75.00 – 95.00.** Author collection

Another great don-lin enameled and articulated Western pin of a blooming cactus in a Mexican pot, 3½" tall, **$35.00 – 45.00.** Author collection

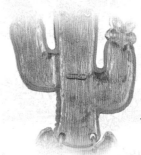

Reverse view of pin showing signature.

Contemporary Jewelry

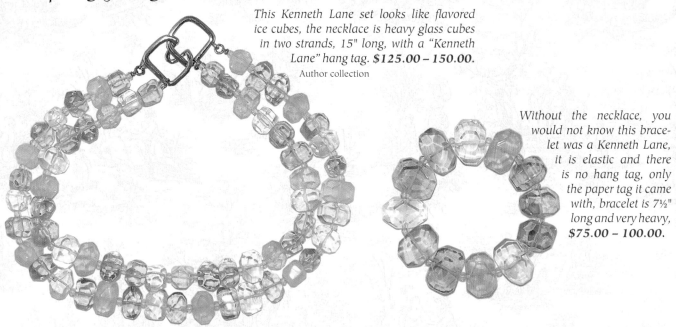

This Kenneth Lane set looks like flavored ice cubes, the necklace is heavy glass cubes in two strands, 15" long, with a "Kenneth Lane" hang tag. **$125.00 – 150.00.**
Author collection

Without the necklace, you would not know this bracelet was a Kenneth Lane, it is elastic and there is no hang tag, only the paper tag it came with, bracelet is 7½" long and very heavy, **$75.00 – 100.00.**

Annie Navetta designs beaded jewelry using vintage beads and components whenever possible. Her website can be found at www.annisoriginalartjewelry.com/. Annie takes special orders such as the fruit jewelry here. I won the bracelet at an auction for charity and Annie made the necklace to match for me. Her designs are gorgeous and some of her work can be seen in my previous books.

Fruit necklace with centerpiece made of vintage fruit glass beads. Necklace is signed with an "Anni" hang tag, and is 19" long, note special hanging fruit at back of clasp. Centerpiece with dangles is 3" long, **$150.00 – 175.00.** Author collection

Here is the stunning fruit design bracelet I won at a charity auction, Annie designed it so that the centerpiece stays anchored on top of your arm, instead of sliding around and ending up underneath. It is a perfect fit, as if it had been designed exclusively for me. Bracelet is 7" long with a push in clasp and the centerpiece is 2" x 2", **$95.00 – 125.00.** Author collection

Here is a fabulous over-loaded charm style bracelet made with all types of glass beads and charms, it has a bird theme with blown glass bird beads scattered throughout, it even has tiny glass bird houses. Bracelet is 8½" long, you need the extra length with all of the charms, and it is nearly 3" wide, or tall as the case may be! **$50.00 – 65.00.** Author collection

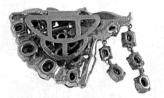

Dress clip with purple and green rhinestones accented with clear stones, clip has two stone dangles on one side, unsigned clip is 3" x 2½" and the longer dangle is 1¾", **$55.00 – 65.00.** Davida Baron collection/Photo courtesy of Davida Baron

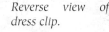

Reverse view of dress clip.

Art glass beads in purple and green make up this simple charm-style bracelet with matching earrings made by Annie Navetta. Bracelet is 7" long and has "Anni" hang tag on it, pierced earrings dangle 1¼", **$25.00 – 55.00.** Author collection

This necklace with the matching bracelet was made for me by Annie Navetta to match the aubergine theme of this volume. This is the set I wore for my author's photograph, and my thanks go to Annie for designing such fabulous jewelry with such an old fashioned look. Necklace has vintage hard glass enamel flowers and leaves, vintage glass German flowers and leaves, new Czech glass flowers and leaves, and vintage rhinestone headpins, with brass ox findings. Necklace chain is vintage Czech faceted lavender opal glass and vintage German lavender opal spiral round beads. Necklace is 18" long with the centerpiece being 3" x 3¼", and it has an "Anni" hang tag, **$195.00 – 255.00.** Annie Navetta collection

I adore these expansion bracelets made by Annie Navetta, this is the one I wore for my author photo. Annie designs these overflowing flower garden bracelets to the customers specifications and I covet every one I have ever seen. This bracelet has flowers of vintage German, Czech, and Japanese glass flowers, and new Czech flowers in lavender, amethyst, and alexandrite glass, while the leaves are all vintage German glass. It is very difficult to measure this type of bracelet but the width goes from 1¼" to 1¾" and the beaded design is over ½" in depth. These expansion bracelets fit most wrists, but Annie can also add links or subtract links for the perfect fit. I warn you though, once you have one of these bracelets, it will not be happy til it has an entire family of flower garden bracelets to join it! **$195.00 – 295.00.** Annie Navetta collection

Memorial to Ian St. Gielar

Ian St. Gielar was a dear, dear friend of mine who passed away in 2007. I don't know that I can tell you how much I miss him. His jewelry designs remain some of my favorites. Below is the press release I prepared as his obituary.

The jewelry world lost a true master with the unexpected death of fashion jewelry designer extraordinaire Ian St. Gielar, who took costume jewelry to a new level of artistry. St. Gielar died March 21, 2007, from a heart attack following a car accident.

Ian St. Gielar worked with vintage beads and findings to create breathtaking jewelry, most of which could be classified as genuine works of art. He went to work for the famed jewelry designer Stanley Hagler in 1989 and helped turn around the Hagler look of muted pearl designs to one of colorful, intricate, and elaborate designs.

He was born April 30, 1953, in Sanok, Poland. He spent many years as a young man traveling through Europe before coming to the United States in 1981. Prior to working with Hagler, St. Gielar was employed by the Diplomat Resort in Florida. The Hollywood, Florida, area was the only home St. Gielar knew in America.

He loved to travel almost as much as he loved tennis. He taught others to play and was an excellent player himself. Designing beautiful jewelry though, was the greatest passion of his life.

St. Gielar was involved in a car accident that eventually prompted a trip to the hospital. It was there St. Gielar suffered a fatal, massive heart attack.

He leaves behind a legacy of gorgeous jewelry designs, worn by stars such as Whoopie Goldberg, Morgan Fairchild, Melanie Griffith, and others. St. Gielar's designs graced many fashion show runways and appeared in numerous fashion magazines, among them such illustrious titles as *Elle, Vogue, Harper's,* and *Shine*. The Corning Museum of Glass includes St. Gielar designs in its collections.

St. Gielar is survived by his wife, Valentina. Collectors and clients alike will be pleased to know that Valentina, who worked with St. Gielar for eight years, will continue his work under the name "Ian Gielar Studio."

This work of art not only looks like it is museum quality, it IS museum quality. This piece is called Bird in Nest and it features over 1,500 hand-applied beads surrounding a carved ivory bird. The bird appears to be a completely carved miniature, she is 1¾" long by nearly 2" tall, with a depth of nearly 2", and she rests on a multicolored beaded nest, encircled by leaves and flowers. Ian Gielar made at least two of these and the one other I know of is being donated to the Corning Museum of Glass. Overall the piece is 5" x 5". It is truly a masterpiece, **$2,000.00+.** Author collection

This whimsical monkey mom and baby pin was featured in my second book, but it deserves to be seen once again. This glorious piece shows the humorous side of designer Ian Gielar but also his great sense of style, as he put together beautifully the overflowing banana leaves and the garden of flowers. The mother and her heart holding baby make you think of the rain forest. The brooch stands 4¾" tall by 3¾" wide. Both the "Hagler" and "Ian St. Gielar" tags are attached, **$500.00 – 650.00.** Author collection

Memorial to Ian St. Gielar

This lovely floral creation has shades of pink and green with flowers and leaves offsetting a lovely large frosted bloom. Pin is 3½" x 2¾" and has both "Hagler" and "Gielar" tags on the back, **$150.00–175.00.** Author collection

A few days after a telephone chat with Ian, I received this totally fabulous, totally outrageous Tutti Frutti Christmas tree pin. Ian Gielar is famous for having added colorful Christmas tree pins to the Hagler inventory and this is one of his marvelous designs. It stands a whopping 4½" tall, and is 3" wide, with a depth over 1". In addition to the hand beading, it also features large glass fruit beads like strawberries, lemons, oranges, and pears. I think it is the most beautiful Christmas tree pin I have ever seen and I am so thrilled to own it that it leans against my computer monitor for me to enjoy on a daily basis. It has both applied tags, **$300.00 – 400.00.** Author collection

This remarkable angel plaque was embellished by Ian, placing the angel in a wildflower garden, there is a paper tag spanning the back saying "designs by Ian. St. Gielar for Stanley Hagler N.Y.C." A very, very rare piece, **$500.00 – 550.00.** Author collection

I was attending a jewelry convention and had spoken on the telephone with Ian, and told him what I was planning to wear to each event. An overnight package arrived with a note in it saying that I should wear this necklace to the formal dinner event. This sensational necklace has just about everything in it and on it; coral beads, art glass beads, a large baroque pearl, porcelain flowers, just too many things to mention. Ian said I could wear this necklace with anything, and he was right. It is another masterpiece of design. Necklace is 19" long with a 4" extender, and the magnificent centerpiece is over 4" wide x 5" tall. Because Ian made this especially for me, it will always remain a true treasure in my collection, **$600.00 – 750.00.** Author collection

Reverse view showing two signature plaques.

Winged brooch in pinks and greens, made as all of his jewelry with impeccable workmanship and a truly artistic eye, like most of the Hagler/Gielar designs, this one has double filigree backing to hide the hand sewn and hand wired work making each piece so beautiful, brooch is 3¾" x 3" and has both signature plaques, **$175.00 – 195.00.** Davida Baron collection/Photo courtesy of Davida Baron

Reverse view showing filigree back and signature plaques.

In 1996, Davida Baron had the opportunity to interview Stanley Hagler and he brought along his star designer, Ian St. Gielar. Shortly after the interview, Ian St. Gielar sent Baron this tremendous brooch in appreciation. It has all vintage rhinestones and crystals in it with purple glass flowers with small pink crystals in the shape of leaves. Hanging from the center is a lovely piece of vintage etched glass with a purple bead on either side. Because St. Gielar made this specially for Baron, it has only the Ian St. Gielar tag on the back. Brooch measures 4½" x 3¾", **$500.00 – 600.00.** Davida Baron collection/Photo courtesy of Davida Baron

Reverse view of brooch.

Artistic masterpiece set by Ian Gielar. We chatted about my upcoming book signing in Dallas and he said he had just the thing to go with my dress. Then he sent me this striking necklace in black and white. The centerpiece, 4" x 3", is next to two hand-wired side adornments which are 2½" x 2" each, necklace is 18" with a 3½" extender, **$550.00 – 650.00** *for the set. Author collection*

And the matching clip earrings, all hand work, 3⅞" x 1⅓", all pieces are signed. Author collection

Brilliant Ideas from the Coro Treasure Chest,
1941, Vogue

Eisenberg Ice, "the famous costume jewelry...,"
1944, Harper's Bazaar

Nettie Rosenstein, "fine bags and individual jewelry...,"
1945, Vogue

Jewels by Trifari,
1945, Vogue

Corocraft, Masterpieces of Fashion Jewelry, 1946, Vogue

Rose Opal by Reja, 1946, Harper's Bazaar

*Jewels by Trifari, Day, Evening,
1946, Harper's Bazaar*

*Magicut jewels, Gems of Inspiration, Mazer Jewels of Elegance,
1948, Vogue*

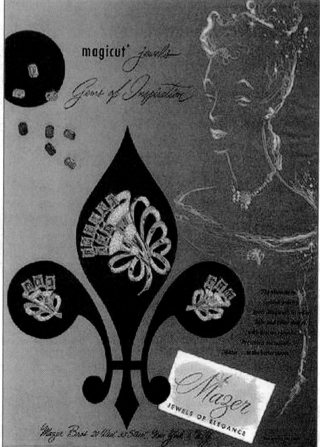

Eisenberg Ice flower holder,
1949, Vogue

Jewels, Haskell,
1951, Harper's Bazaar

Romanesque by Pennino,
1953, Vogue

Jewels by Trifari, royal jewels,
1953, Harper's Bazaar

Pennino original Gala Night,
1954, Vogue

Ecstasy, another original by Pennino, 1955,
Vogue

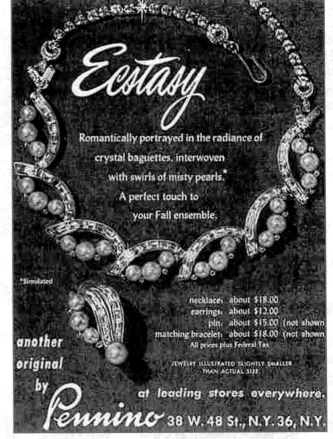

Jewels by Pennino, Falling Leaves, 1956, Vogue

Jewels by Pennino, Floral Cascade, 1956, Vogue

Pins a-la-mode! obviously by Triafri, 1958, Vogue

Persian Petals by Albert Weiss, 1959, Harper's Bazaar

Vendome, rings, 1969, Vogue

A tremendous amount of websites now offer vintage costume jewelry. Some of the very best offer more than just jewelry for sale, many offer free educational tools. *Volume One* offered 35 websites and *Volume 2* offered 38 websites. This chapter continues with completely different websites. In addition to the ones listed, you can find many more vintage costume jewelry sites at larger "stores" such as Tias.com and RubyLane.com. These sites are both important, but their individual sites are too numerous to mention. They are easy to navigate when you are ready to "shop" their "stores."

Each website was given the same questionnaire, which follows. Many of these website owners belong to one or more of these groups which will be abbreviated in the listing: the Vintage Fashion & Costume Jewelry club is listed as VFCJ, Discovering Juliana Jewelry is DJJ, Jewelcollect is listed as JC, Collecting Miriam Haskell is CMH, and JewelryRing is listed as JR. Information about these groups follows the website listings for those wishing to join or to obtain additional information. Use this section also if you are trying to sell some jewelry, each site lists what they are actively seeking to aid your search for a buyer for your jewelry.

Many of the sites listed have weekly or monthly newsletters that are free. Visit each site and sign up for those you are interested in, and get advance notice of sales and updates.

Because of the economic times, some of these long-term sites may have disappeared by the time the book has been published. I apologize for any confusion this may cause.

The Questionnaire

Date your site started.
Owners' names.
What exactly do you carry?
What do you consider to be your specialty?
Is there any costume jewelry you are actively seeking?
Would you like sellers to contact you; if so, how?
Does your site have a buyer's wish list?
Do you belong to any professional organizations?
Do you do appraisals?

Is there any additional information you would like included? Please use this section to "chat" with your future buyers to either tell them about yourself or what makes you or your website of special interest to them.

Treasures-In-Time

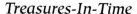

Owner: Carol Bell
www.treasures-in-time.com
Est. May 2001
Offering: Vintage, collectible, and designer signed costume jewelry plus vintage accessories including compacts and purses.
Seeking: I am always buying designer signed jewelry.
Contact: I can be contacted at carol@treasures-in-time.com or 281-610-2897.
Organizations: VFCJ, JC, and JR
No appraisals.
Comments: I have a personal collection of 1910 – 1930 headbands, sew-ons, and head-pieces. I'm always looking for more.

Mary Ann, Mary Ann

Owner: Mary Ann Docktor-Smith
www.maryannmaryann.com
Est. 2005
Offering: Unique and beautiful vintage jewelry in a wide variety of styles and price ranges. Also offering artisan jewelry designs featuring new/old stock vintage components.
Specialty: Vintage pieces dating from the 1930s through the 1980s, signed and unsigned, and bracelets of all types.
Seeking: Vintage pieces in need of repair and restoration, especially large lots.
Contact: maryann@maryannmaryann.com
Organizations: VFCJ, JR, JC, DJJ
Appraisals available.
Comments: Vintage jewelry repair and restoration services are offered; please inquire. I have extensive expertise in Florenza jewelry designs and the history of its designer, Dan Kasoff. My website is updated on a regular basis with additional items being added each week. You'll also find interesting reference information about sword-motif, "partridge in a pear tree," and eagle pins and brooches. My primary goal is to have my customers enjoy doing business with me as much as I enjoy working with them!

Kim Loves Vintage

Owner: Kim DeWitt Paff
www.KimsVintage.com
www.KimLovesVintage.com
Est. 2002

Offering: A large selection of quality vintage costume jewelry, specializing in vintage Bakelite jewelry, new designer Bakelite jewelry, rhinestone jewelry, designer signed and unsigned vintage costume jewelry, Victorian and vintage fine jewelry, period jewelry, antiques, purses, and accessories.

Specialty: Quality vintage costume jewelry and Bakelite, new designer Bakelite.

Seeking: Hobé, Bakelite, Kunio Matsumoto by Trifari.

Contact: KimLovesVintage@gmail.com or call me at 352-238-4933.

Organizations: VFCJ and JC

Appraisals available.

Comments: www.KimsVintage.com is proud to host GingersJewels, a page featuring vintage European designer jewelry from the personal collection of Ginger Moro, internationally known author, actress and collector. Moro is the author of *European Designer Jewelry*. Access Gingers Jewels from the left hand menu of the main page of the website.

My retail location is in Brooksville, Florida – 31 South Main Street inside the Antique Sampler Antique Mall. Open 6 days per week, 10am – 5pm. I am available the third Saturday of the month in the shop or by appointment. I am always buying entire estates or by the piece. I also do repairs and restorations to all types of vintage jewelry, in particular enamel restoration. I make original design Bakelite jewelry using vintage Bakelite components and make rhinestone collage jewelry. I am also currently experimenting with making "altered" clothing using vintage clothing and jewelry components. I hope to have them on my website by summer of 2008.

James Katz Vintage Costume Jewelry and Accessories

Owner: James Katz
www.james-katz.com
Est. 2006
Offering: Vintage costume jewelry & accessories.
Specialty: WWII era jewelry.
Seeking: WWII vintage sterling jewelry.
Organizations: JC & JR
No appraisals.

Eclectic Vintage

Owner: Jan Gaughan
www.eclecticvintage.com
Est. 1998
Offering: Vintage costume jewelry and collectibles.
Specialty: Florenza specialist, Forbidden Fruit, Kenneth Lane.
Seeking: Florenza, Forbidden Fruit.
Contact: info@eclecticvintage.com
Organizations: JC, VFCJ, JR, DJJ
No appraisals.

Comments: With over 25 years in the business and on the internet since 1998, we are proud to offer an eclectic mix of quality vintage jewelry, antiques, and collectibles. We successfully operated a site on the Ruby Lane Antique Mall for 6½ years when they first opened in 1998. Our independent site opened in 2005 offering the same quality jewelry that we provided on Ruby Lane. We are pleased to offer easy view galleries and image event albums showcasing some of our specialties. To name a few we feature Florenza, Forbidden Fruit, Kenneth Lane, D&E, and more. We also provide a research information page on our website for collectors as well as dealers. Eclectic Vintage strives for excellent customer service and hope to add you to our long list of satisfied customers. Visit our site and read what some of our customers have to say about us: www.eclecticvintage.com/comments.html

Joan's Jewels & Collectibles

Owner: Joan M. Redden
www.joansjewelsandcollectibles.com
Est. December 1999
Offering: Vintage collectible jewelry, estate jewelry, vintage fashions & accessories, original jewelry designs by JMR Originals, contemporary designer jewelry, and selective collectibles.

Specialty: Crystal rhinestone jewelry, particularly 1940s – 1950s.

Seeking: Vintage crystal rhinestone brooches and earrings.

Contact: joanredden@verizon.net
941-355-9171
Joan M Redden
P.O. Box 462, Tallevast, FL 34270-0462.

Organizations: JC and VFCJ
No appraisals.

Comments: I have a long relationship with costume jewelry. Each item is selected with care and pride. My number one concern is a pleasant and carefree shopping experience for you. A chance for you and yours to own a piece of the past. I do offer gift wrapping and a layaway plan is available upon request for items over $100.00.

Past and Present Jewelry

Owner: Diane Hanselman
www.pastandpresentjewelry.com
Est. December 2000
Offering: Contemporary and vintage costume jewelry.
Specialty: Most knowledgeable about Eisenberg, Trifari, Art Deco.
Seeking: Trifari and a few D&E pieces
Contact: ppj@awcmail.com
Organizations: VFCJ, JC, JR, DJJ, CMH
No appraisals.

Comments: I have been in business for 15 years and been a collector for 20. I do shows as well as the website and have had a brick and mortar store from 1992 to 2007. We aim to sell the best jewelry we can find, in excellent condition and at reasonable prices and are quite knowledgeable about the contemporary jewelry market as well as vintage. We carry new Eisenberg, Kenneth Jay Lane, Dorothy Bauer, and also specialize in prom, bridal, and pageant jewelry. I am always happy to do special orders and help you find what you are seeking.

Kristy Lee Jewelry

Owner: Kristy Lee
www.kristyleejewelry.com
Est. October 2006
Offering: Vintage, costume, contemporary, and original jewelry designs by Kristy Lee. I also offer a small selection of antiques and collectibles.
Speciality: My own "one of a kind" beaded jewelry, handcrafted and signed by me, Kristy Lee.

Contact: kristylee@centurytel.net
Organizations: JC and VFCJ.
No appraisals.

Comments: I focus on quality merchandise and friendly customer service because of my own ebullient passion for jewelry and the desire to share it with others.

Hag Jewels

Owner: Helen Anne Gilson
www.HagJewels.com
Est. 2007
Offering: Previously worn, gently loved vintage and contemporary jewelry.
Specialty: Bargains and marriages — Our Motto is "HAGJewels — Where Looking Good Is Easy!" because we will have a number of mix and match sets.
Seeking: Marcasites and Taxco.
Contact: Info@HagJewels.com
Organizations: JR
No appraisals.

Comments: I first fell in love with jewelry when I became a Premier Designs Independent sales consultant. I learned a lot about jewelry and started collecting information in the eBay Jewelry and Gemstone Forum and in the Yahoo group Jewelry Ring. The members in both areas were just amazing in their depth of knowledge and willingness to share it. We all are on some kind of budget and are all busy in our lives. I wanted a site that helps answer the need in both groups and at both ends of the spectrum. We have tried to make looking good easy and quick. We have an extensive resource library to browse for research. In order for me to become more knowledgeable, I've collected this compendium of information and make it publicly available to all of you as well. If you have or know of a site you would like to add, please email me. You will want to keep HAGJewels on your favorite links bar!

Great Vintage Jewelry

Owner: Veronica McCullough
www.greatvintagejewelry.com
Est. 1998
Offering: A large online collection of antique, vintage, and retro jewelry.
Specialty: Art Deco, retro modern, vintage copper & silver, designer costume jewelry, bridal, and pearl jewelry,

Damascene, Bohemian Eames era, and hippie jewelry. Buyer's wish list.

Seeking: Signed copper and copper enamel jewelry.

Contact: info@greatvintagejewelry.com

No appraisals.

Comments: Vintage jewelry restoration, conversions, and enamel restoration. Worldwide shipping. Free US shipping, free US insurance, and free gift wrapping. Wholesale to the public. Online jewelry research, blog, and jewelry forum. Advanced user friendly website.

The following websites were found in my first two books, and are updated here, for your convenience.

Barbara B. Woods Vintage and Costume Jewelry
www.bwoodantiques.com

N&N Vintage Costume Jewelry
www.JewelMuseum.com

Eclectica
www.Eclecticala.com

Morning Glory Antiques
www.morninggloryantiques.com

Plastic Fantastic
www. plasticfantastic.com

Liz Jewel
www.lizjewel.com

Jan's Jewels and More
www.jansjewels.com

Emerald City Vintage Costume Jewelry
www.emcity.com

Azillion SPARKLZ Vintage Costume Jewelry & Fine Estate Jewelry
www.sparklz.com

Bijoutree's Jeweled Forest
www.christmastreepins.com

Illusion Jewels
www.illusionjewels.com

Rhinestone Rainbow
www.rhinestonerainbow.com

B'sue Boutiques
www.bsueboutiques.com

Aurora Bijoux Costume Jewelry
www.aurorabijoux.com

Valerie Gedziun – Designer Costume Jewelry
www.valerieg.com

Whiskey Creek Jewels
www.whiskey-creek.net

Carole Tanenbaum Vintage Collection
www.truefaux.com

Just Jewelry
www.jstjewelry.com

Eureka, I Found It! Antiques and Collectibles
www.eureka-I-found-it.com

Sue's Jewels
www.SuesJewels.com

Bakelite Boutique
www.bakeliteboutique.com

Garden Party Collection
www.costumejewel.com

Antique and Costume Jewelry Replacement Stones
www.mrstones.com

ChicAntiques
www.ChicAntiques.com

The Family Jools
www.familyjools.com

Jazzle Dazzle
www.jazbot.com

Shop Vintage Treasures
www.vintagejewelry.com

Deja – Voodoo
www.deja-voodoo.com

Annis Original Art Jewelry
www.annisoriginalartjewelry.com

Cristobal
www. cristobal.co.uk

Bitz of Glitz
www.bitzofglitz.com

The Lush Life Antiques
www.thelushlifeantiques.com

Pretty Snazzy
www.prettysnazzy.com

Edgewater Vintage Jewels
www.EdgewaterVintageJewels.com

Vintage Jewelry Online
www.vintagejewelryonline.com

Yesterdays Jewels
www.yesterdaysjewels.com

Granny's Jewelry Box
www.grannysjewelrybox.com

Sassy Classics Vintage Jewelry, Antique
Jewelryand Estate Jewelry
www.sassyclassics.com

Let's Get Vintage
www.letsgetvintage.com

Amazing Adornments
www.amazingadornments.com

Lasting Values Vintage Jewelry
www.lastingvalues.com

Past Perfection Vintage Costume Jewelry
www.pastperfection.com
www.rubylane.com/shops/pastperfection

Michelle's Vintage Jewelry
www.michellesvintagejewelry.com

Forgotten Romance Collectible Costume Jewelry
and Accessories
www.forgotten-romance.com

Jennifer Lynn's Timeless Jewelry
www.jltimelessjewelry.com

Lady Frog's Vintage Jewelry
www.ladyfrog-vintage-jewelry.com

The Glitter Box Vintage Collectible Designer Jewelry
www.glitterbox.com

Antiques by Evelyn
www.antiquesbyevelyn.com

Capricious Crowns & Jewels
www.capriciouscrowns.com

Remember When Vintage
www.rememberwhenvintage.com

Broadwater Rose Jewels
www.broadwaterrosejewels.com

Forever Vogue Vintage Jewelry & Artwork
www.forevervoguevintagejewelry.com

Vintage Costume Jewelry Dot Com
www.vintagecostumejewelry.com

Annie Sherman Vintage Jewelry
www.anniesherman.com

Here are a few shops you may like to visit at Ruby
Lane found at
www.rubylane.com

Sande Katttau at KATTSLAIR
www.rubylane.com/shops/kattslair

Websites

Claudia Roach at The Pink Lady
www.rubylane.com/shops/thepinklady

Lisa B. Boydstun at Gingerbread Farm Antiques
and Vintage Jewelry
www.rubylane.com/shops/gingerbreadfarm

Mariann Katz at Mariann Katz Original Designs
and Vintage Costume Jewelry
www.rubylane.com/shops/mariannkatz

Cindy Amirkhan at A TWINKLE in TIME Vintage
Jewelry & Accessories
www.rubylane.com/shops/atwinkleintime

Linn Alber at Linn's Collection At Rainbows' End
www.rubylane.com/shops/linnscollection
atrainbowsend

Lorna Breshears at Jewelry Addiction
www.rubylanea/shops/jewelryaddiction

TACE
Terri Friedman at Rhumba!
tace.com/vendors/rhumba.html

Special Interest

There are several clubs available to those interested in vintage costume jewelry, including several online groups. One online group that is gathering a plethora of members sharing information and photographs is The Jewelry Ring found on Yahoo Groups. Please read about this group.

THE JEWELRY RING

The Jewelry Ring (JR) is a comprehensive, easy-to-navigate, friendly, and unique online email discussion group for vintage and costume jewelry enthusiasts, experts, historians, collectors, and dealers. Members are encouraged to join in JR's indepth discussions and to participate in research about important periods, styles, fashion history, and designers. JR's membership includes many published authors and jewelry experts who actively participate and lend their knowledge and expertise to formal and informal JR group discussions. Individuals at all levels of experience and knowledge are welcome, and actively participate in JR posts, discussions, contests, and activities.

Special Jewelry Ring features and group activities include:
Daily Member Email Posts, Chat of the Week, Thursday Shop Day, JR Mall, JR Artisan Mall, JR Blog, JR Member Photo Album, Jewel of the Month Club, Book Reviews, Request for Identification Album, Wednesday Challenge, Finding mates to singles earrings, completing sets.

To inquire about joining the Jewelry Ring, please send an email to Judi Bollan at jewelryjudi@yahoo.com. The JR website address is http://groups.yahoo.com/group/Jewelry_Ring/

Other groups of interest:
JewelCollect — to join, go to www.lizjewel.com and follow the instructions.
Collecting Miriam Haskell — go to http://groups.yahoo.com/group/CollectingMiriamHaskell/ and follow the instructions.
Discovering Juliana Jewelry — http://groups.yahoo.com/group/discoveringjulianajewelry/ and follow the instructions.
Vintage Fashion and Costume Jewelry — VFCJ — contact Lucille Tempesta, P.O. Box 265, Glen Oaks, NY 11004

THE VINTAGE JEWELRY

As a vintage costume jewelry enthusiast, I love finding shops that are treasure troves of jewelry. One such shop opened up in 2007 in historic Greer, South Carolina. The Vintage Jewelry store is owned and operated by Peter Tripp and Harold Baker and it is filled to the rafters with vintage costume jewelry and fashions including hats and purses. Their artistry and expertise make a visit to this shop a great experience. If you have the opportunity to travel to upstate South Carolina, Greer is located between Greenville and Spartanburg and is very easy to find. The Vintage Jewelry store is located at 200 Trade Street, Greer, SC (864) 877-3337.

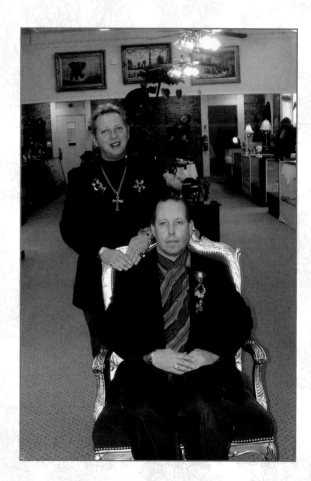

This photo shows Peter Tripp (seated in one of Tammy Faye Baker's throne chairs) and Harold Baker in their store between showcases filled with vintage costume jewelry.

Bibliography

Baker, Lillian. *Fifty Years of Collectible Fashion Jewelry*. Collector Books, 1986.

Ball, Joanne Dubbs and Torem, Dorothy Hehl. *Costume Jewelers, The Golden Age of Design*. Schiffer Publishing, 1990.

_____. *Masterpieces of Costume Jewelry*. Schiffer Publishing, 1996.

Carroll, Julia. *Collecting Costume Jewelry 202*. Collector Books, 2007.

Cera, Deanna Farnetti. *Amazing Gems*. Harry Abrahms Inc., 1995.

Christie's East Couture Jewels: The Designs of Robert Goossens, auction catalog, Wednesday 15 November 2000.

DeLizza, Frank R. *DeLizza and Elster, Memoirs of a Fashion Jewelry Manufacturer*. DeLizza Publications, 2007.

Dolan, Maryanne. *Collecting Rhinestone and Colored Jewelry 4th Edition*. Books Americana, 1998.

Flood, Kathy. *Warman's Costume Jewelry Figurals, Identification and Price Guide*. Krause Publications, 2007.

Gordon, Angie. *Twentieth Century Costume Jewelry*. Adasia International, 1990.

Miller, Harrice Simons. *Costume Jewelry Identification and Price Guide, 2nd Edition*. Avon Books, 1994.

Moro, Ginger H. *European Designer Jewelry*. Schiffer, 1995.

Parry, Karima. *Bakelite Bangles Price & Identification Guide*. Krause Publications, 1999.

_____. *Bakelite Pins*. Schiffer Publishing, 2001.

Pullée, Caroline. *20th Century Jewelry*. JG Press, 1997.

Rezazadeh, Fred. *Costume Jewelry, A Practical Handbook & Value Guide*. Collector Books, 1998.

Simonds, Cherri. *Collectible Costume Jewelry Identification & Values*. Collector Books, 1997.

Time-Life. *The Encyclopedia of Collectibles, Inkwells to Lace*. Time-Life Books, 1997.

Tolkien, Tracy and Wilkinson, Henrietta. *A Collector's Guide to Costume Jewelry*. Firefly Books, 1997.

Index

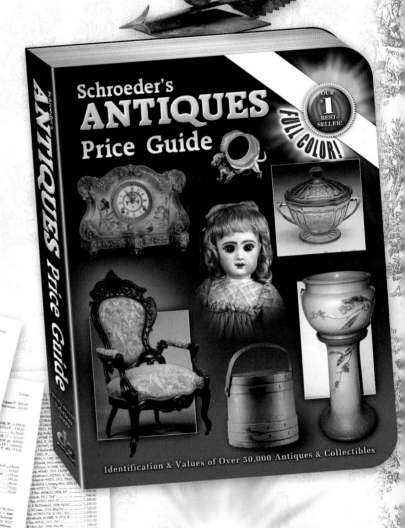